Visitor Travels
a day away

Joseph Fleming

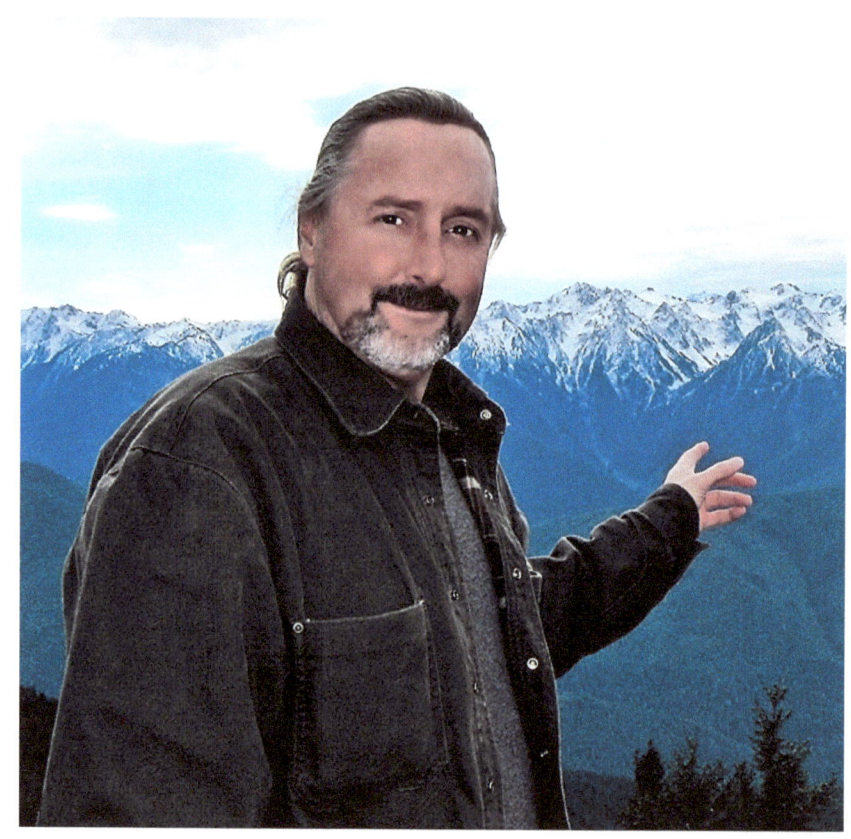

Joseph Fleming

Original Fine Art Photographs

Decades of being around accomplished talent producing absolutely phenomenal quality work has taught that we are capable of greatness. It is possible to meet our destiny and become it. Experiencing excellence done with such apparent ease and humble selfless gratification is the motivation for this photography. Most important was having the freedom

Being colorblind gives an advantage when composing black & white… less confusion.
This special collection selected from thousands of captures. All images were framed
in the camera and presented without edits, genuine as seen through the lens.
RAW conversion applied by proprietary panchromatic process.

Limited edition prints available from original source files.

info@ BEACHNOISE.com

0125

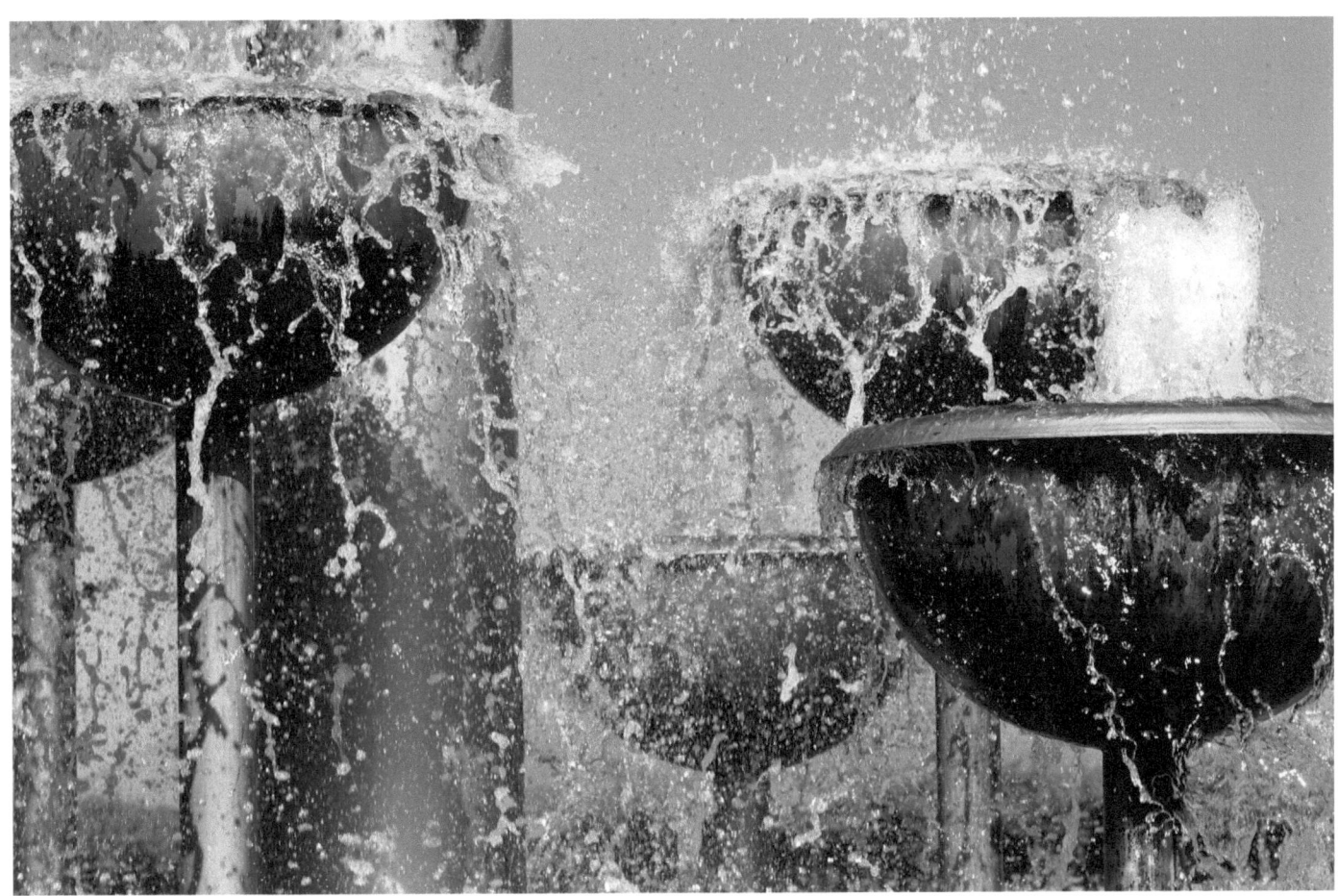

0354

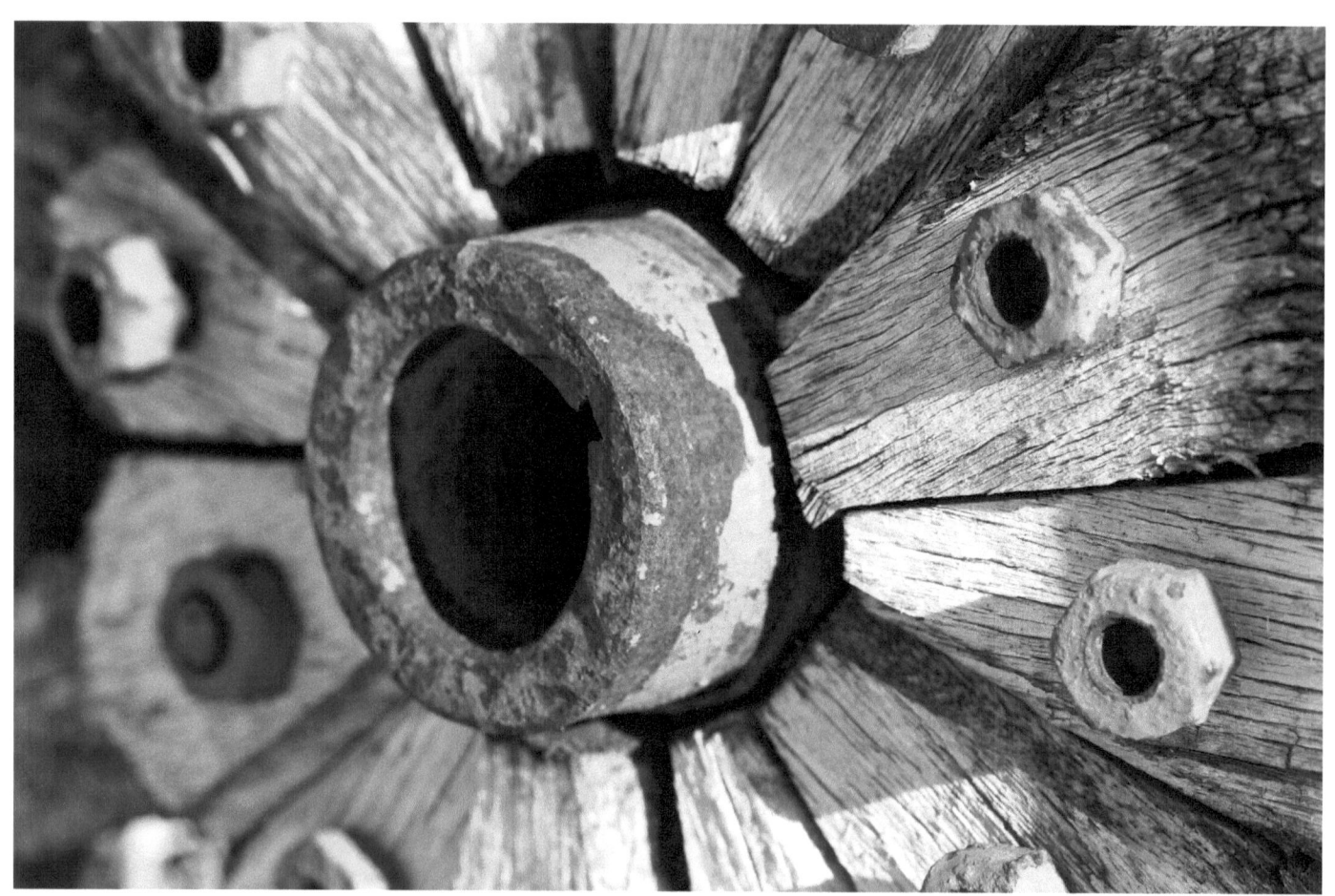

0437

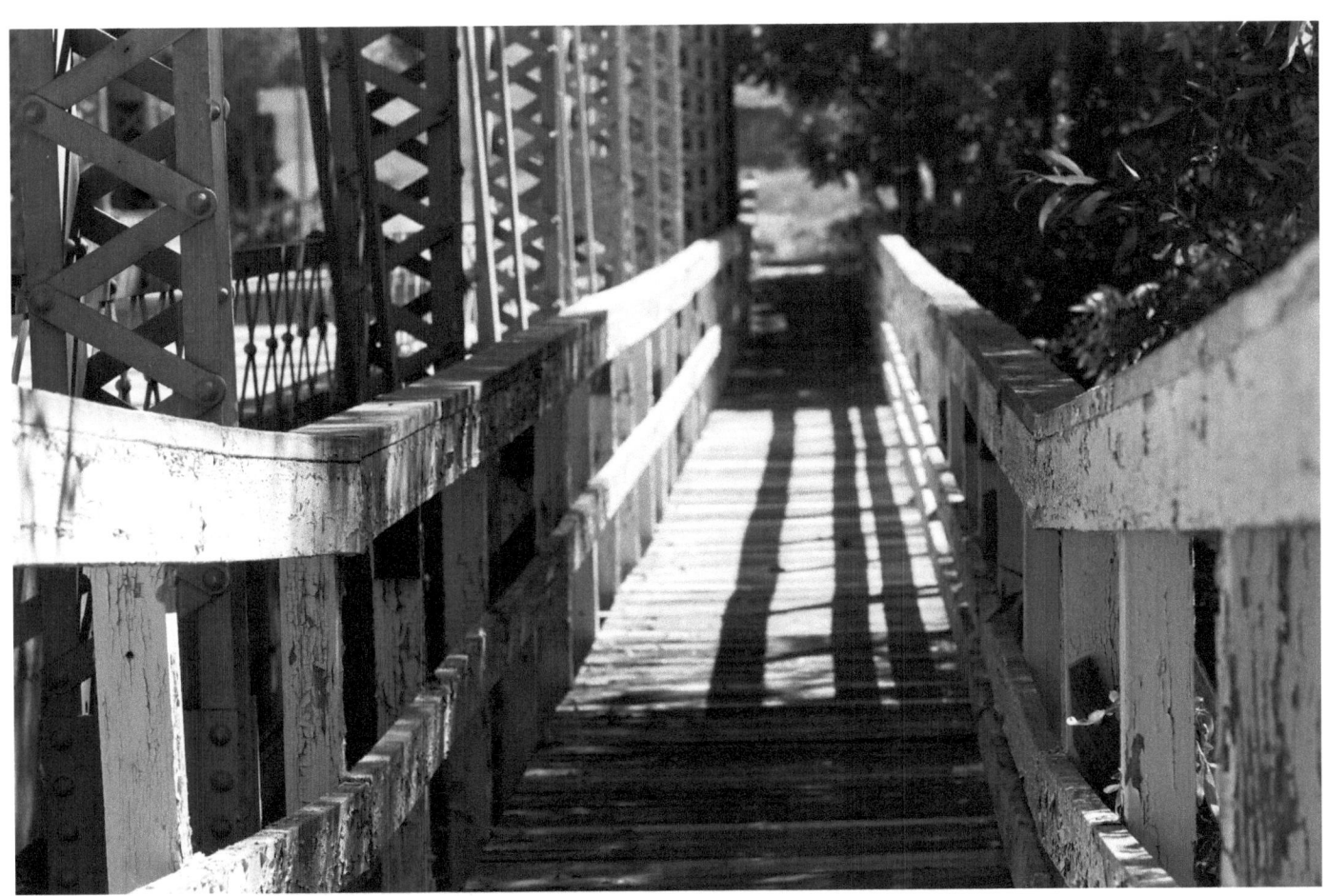

0503

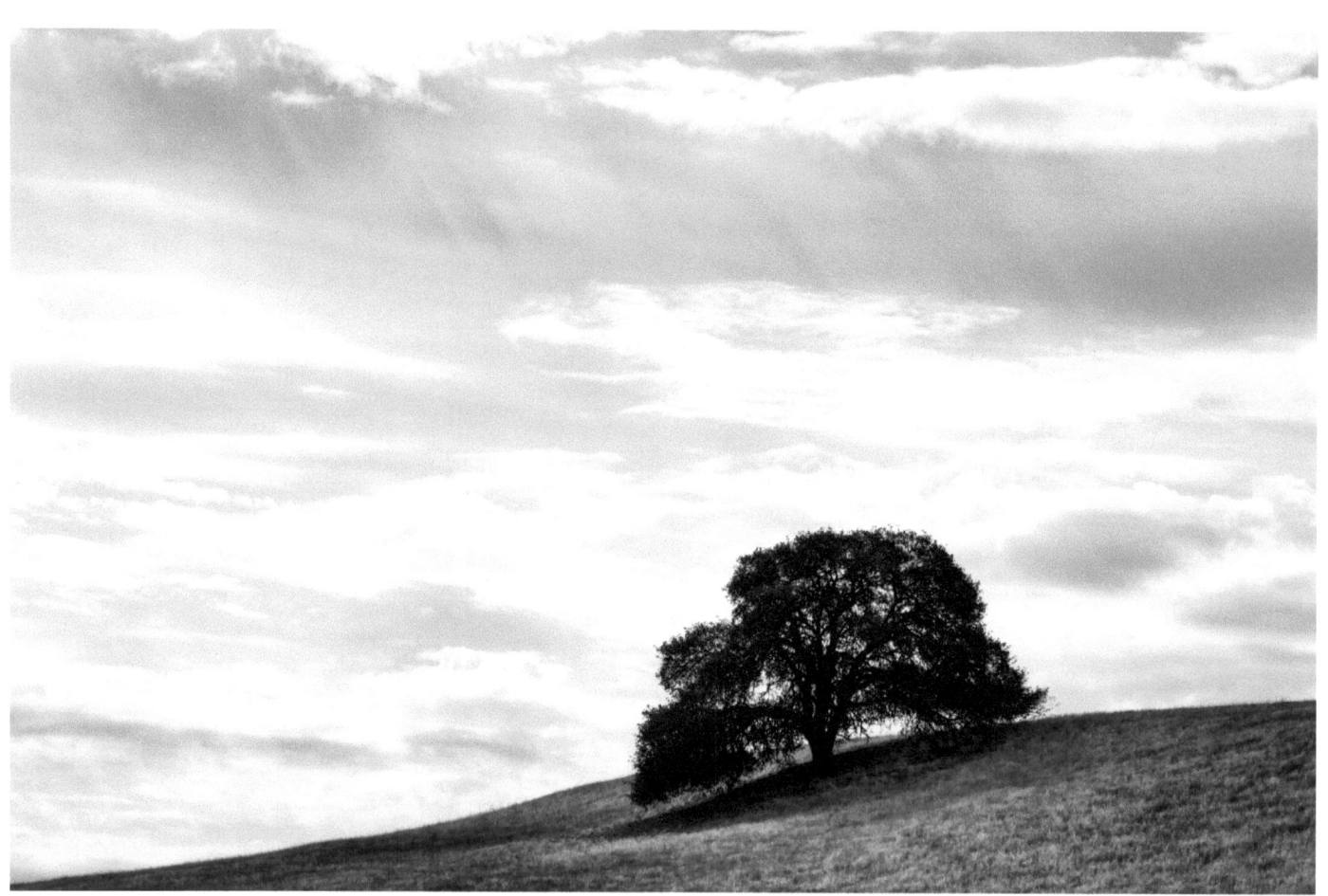

0531

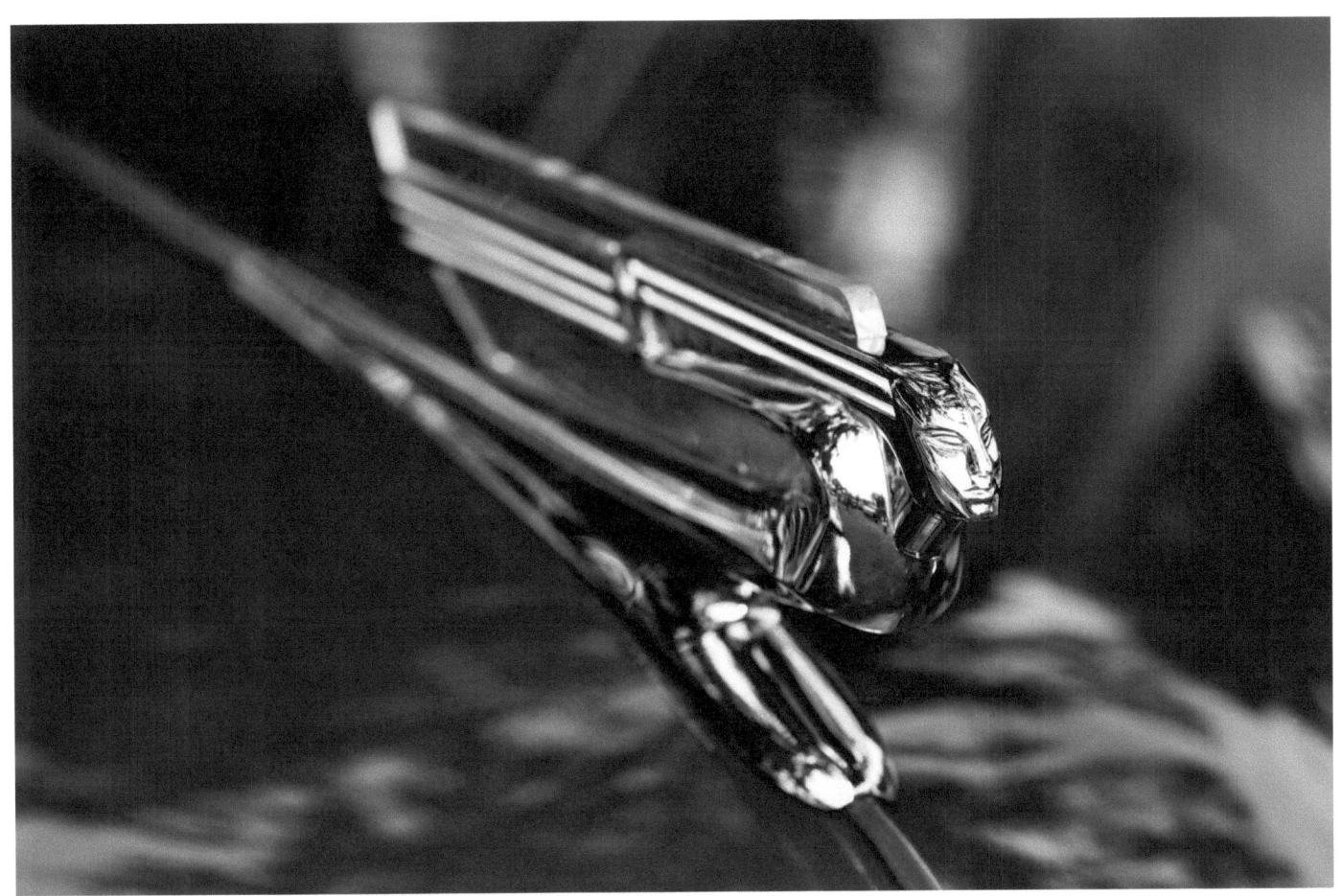

0705

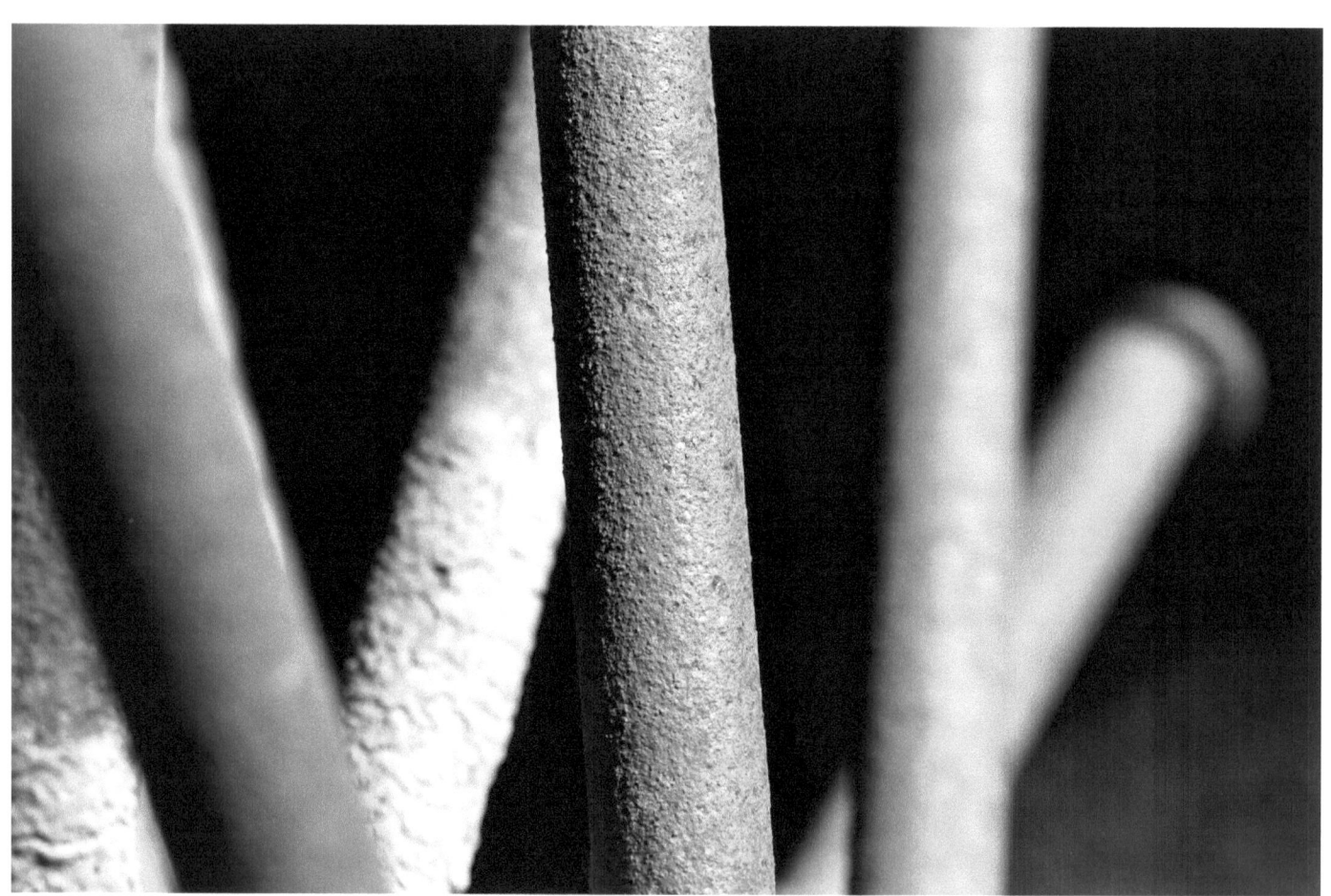

0780

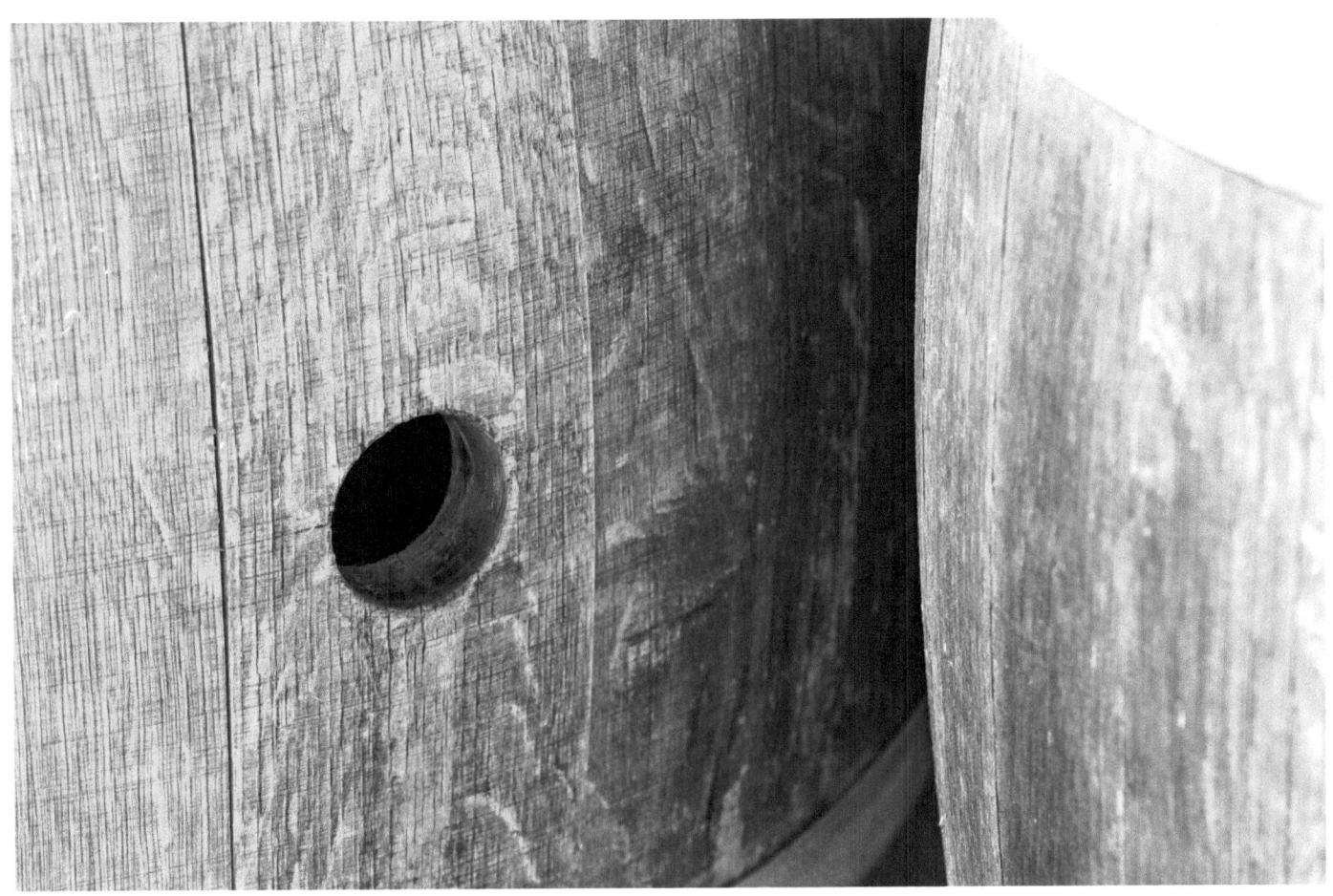

0826

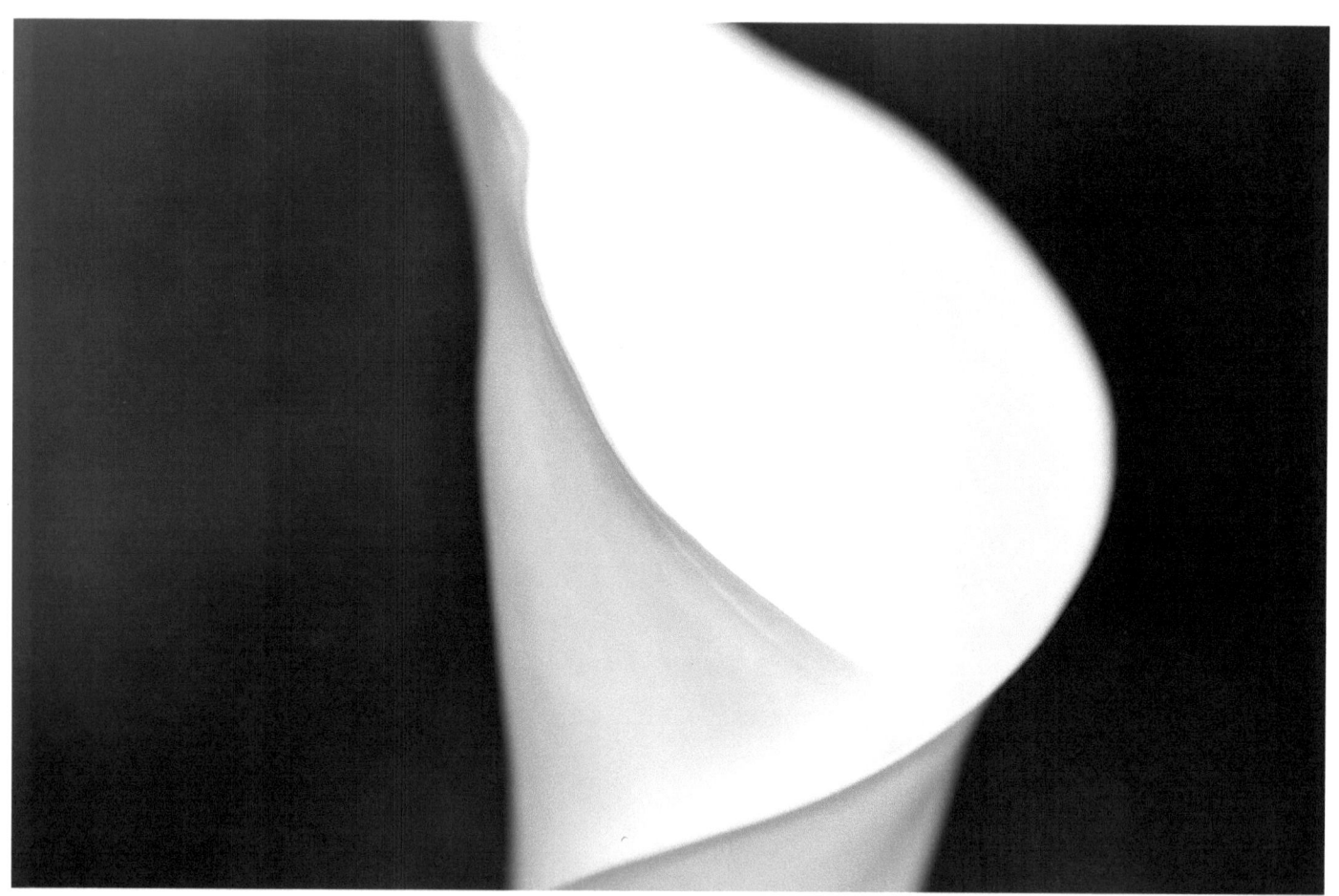

0920

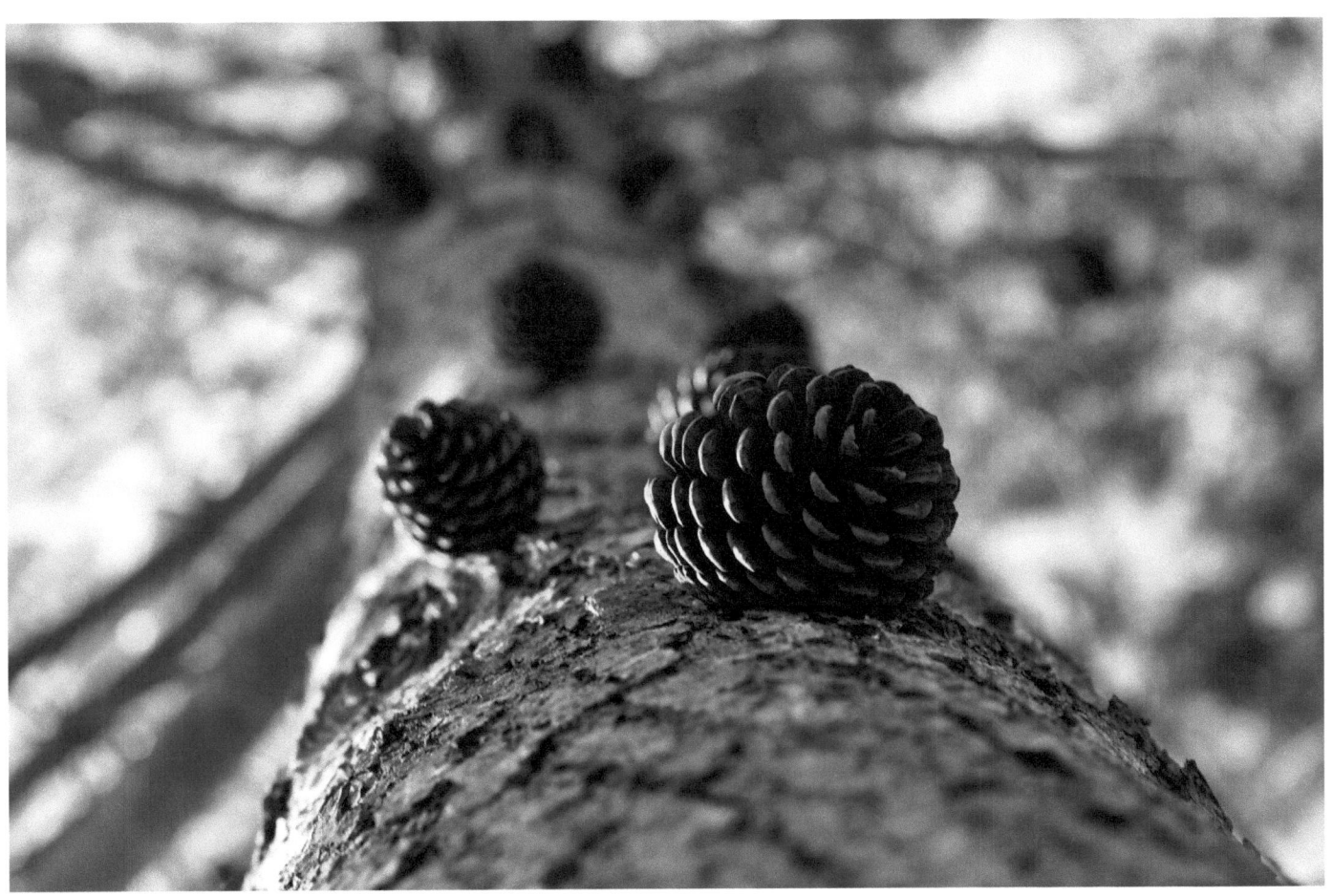

0938

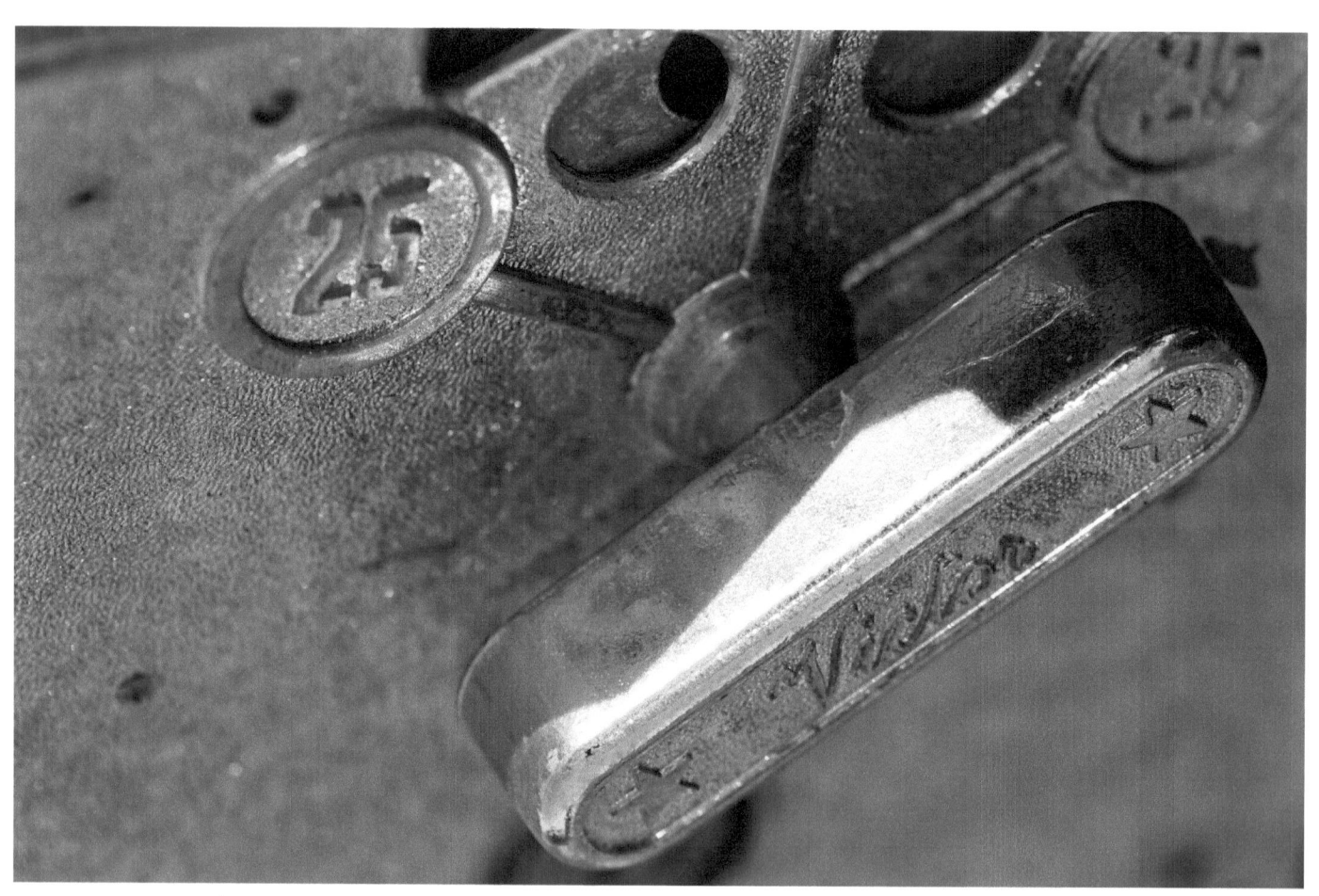

1085

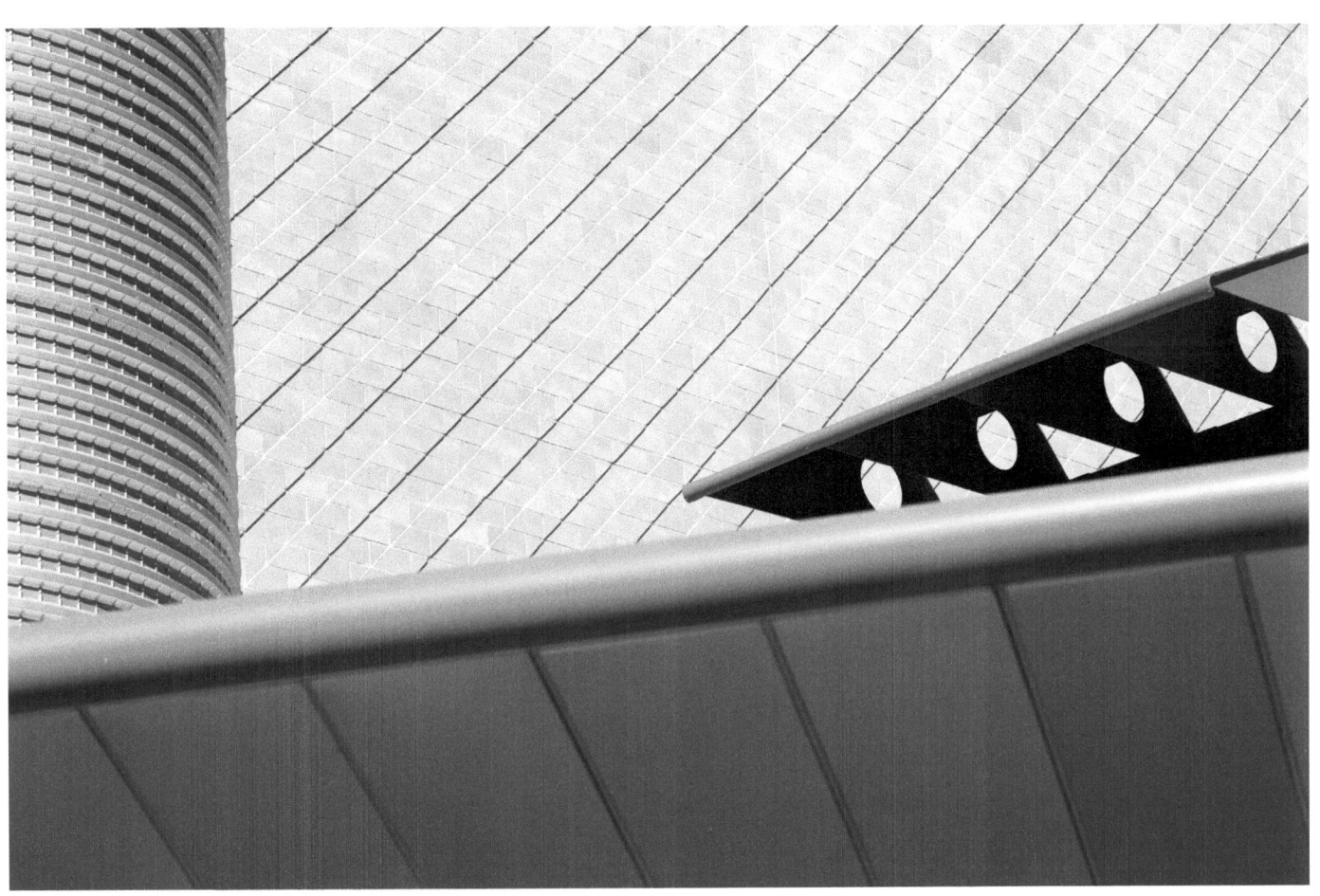

1088

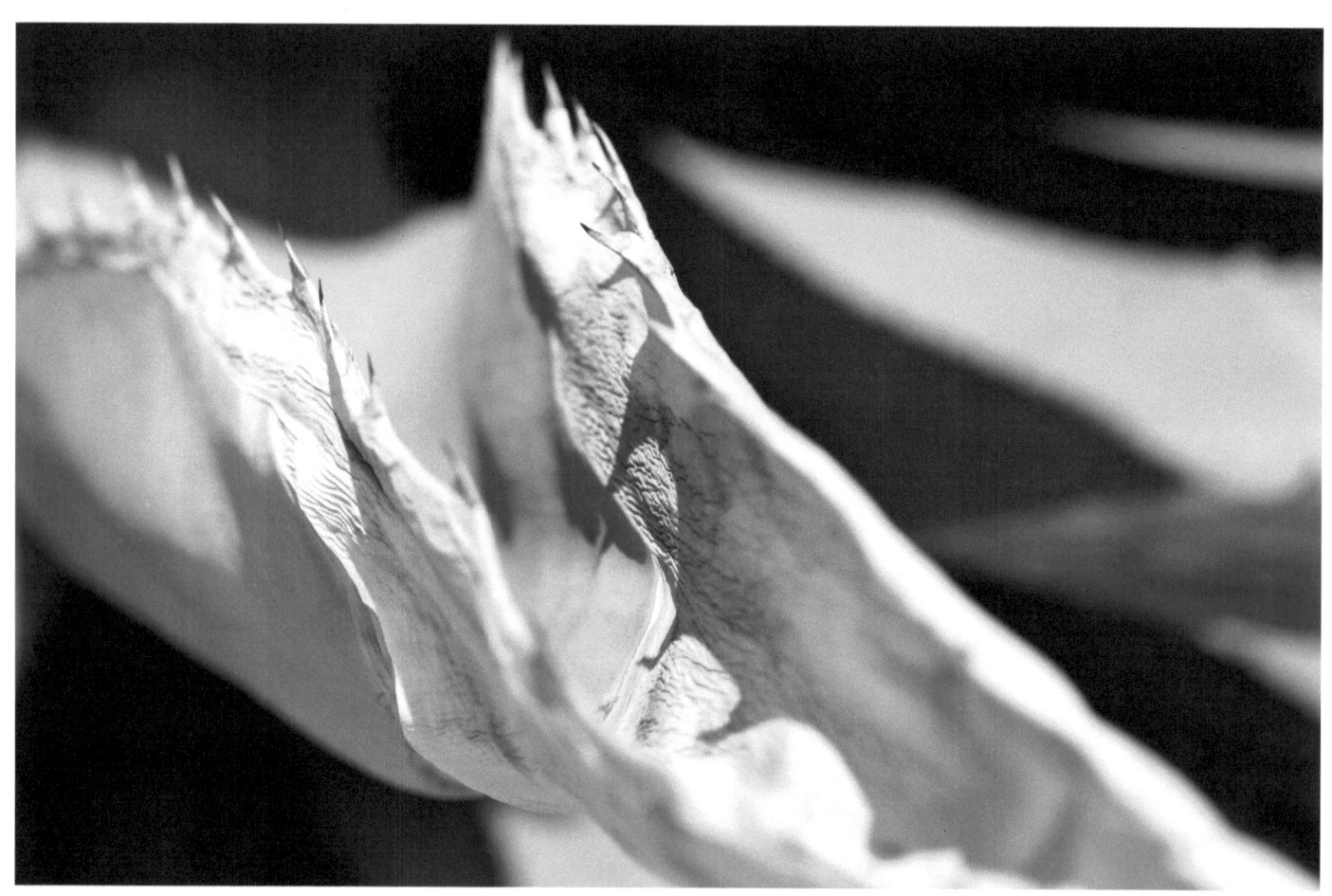

1581

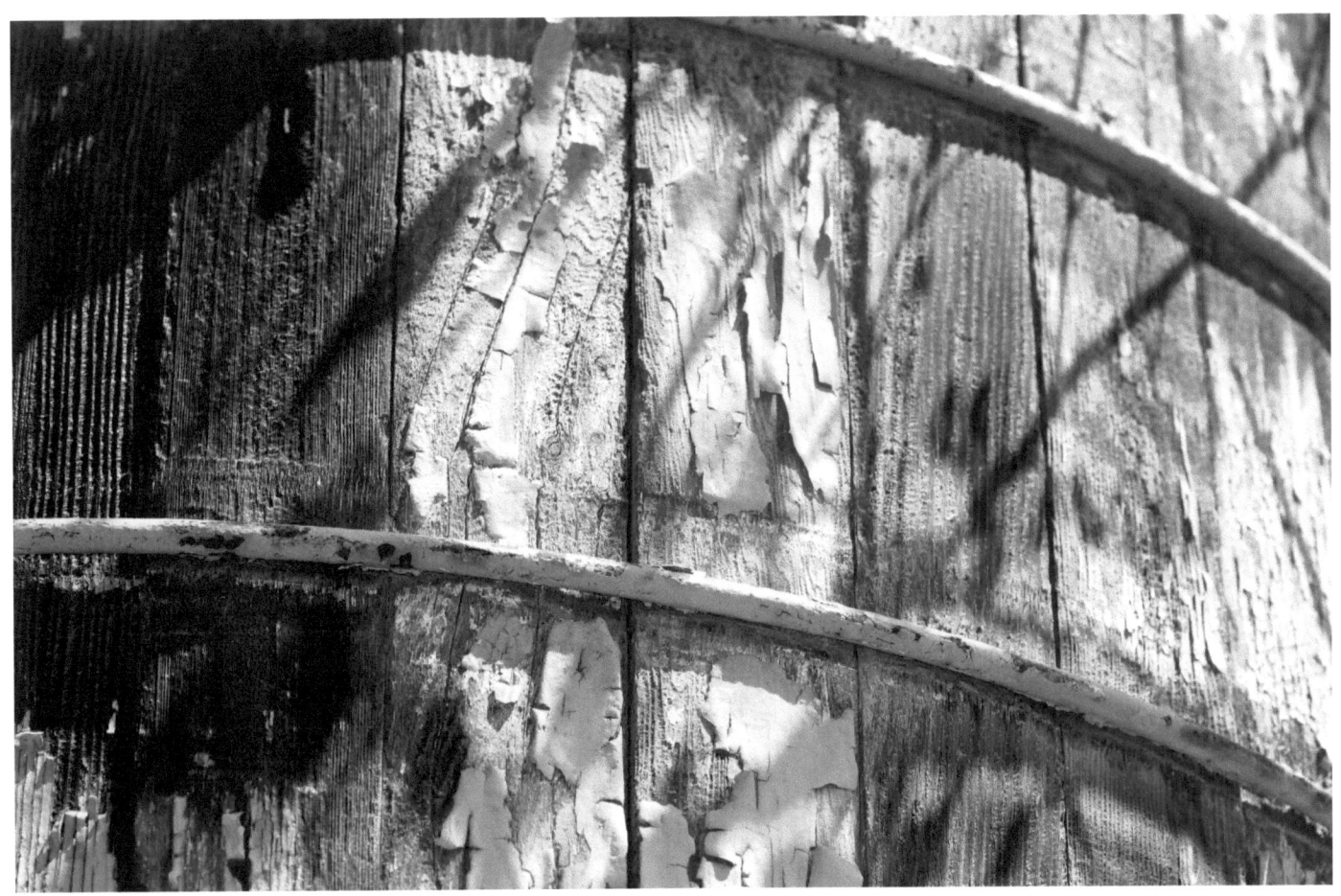

1608

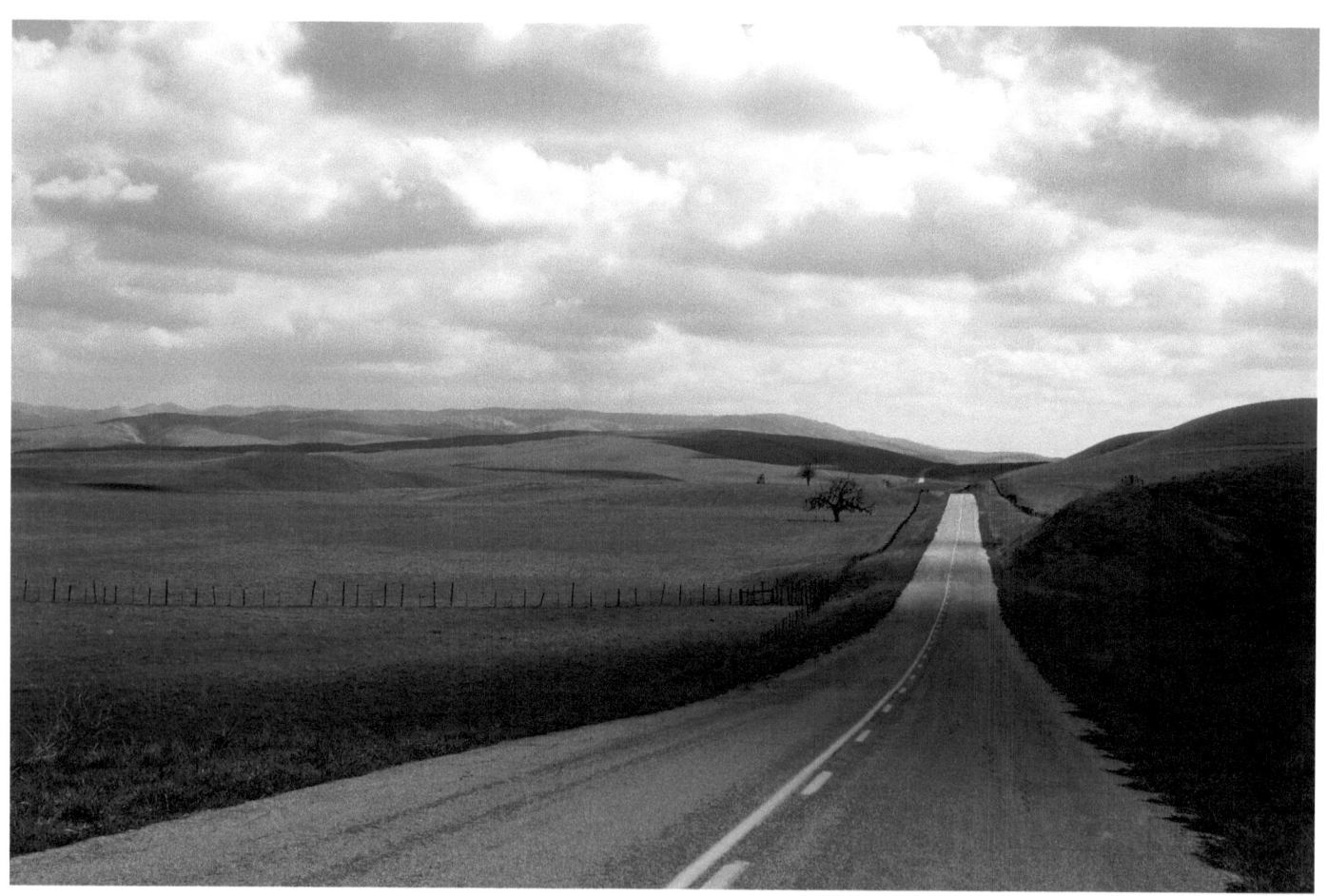

1784

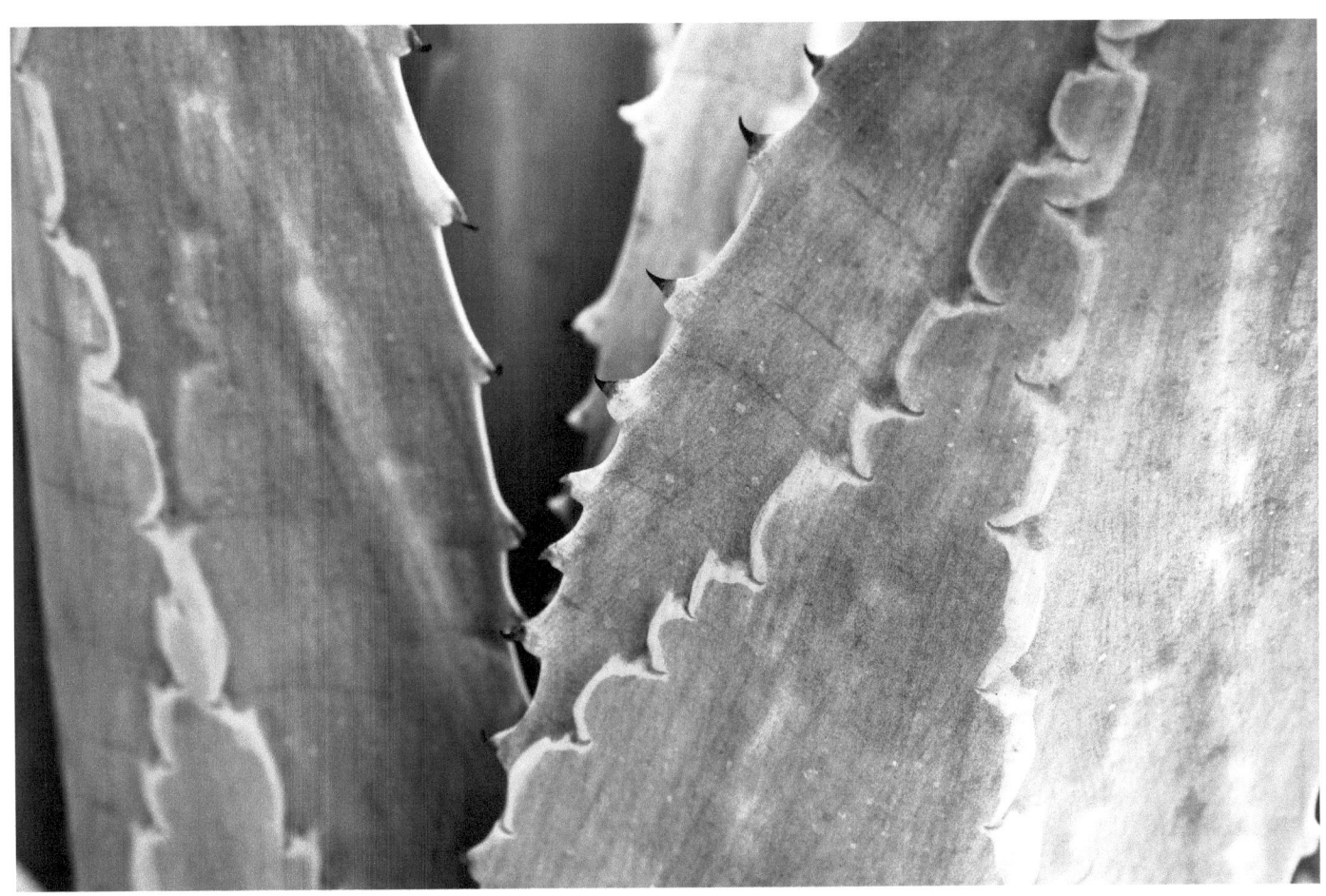

1976

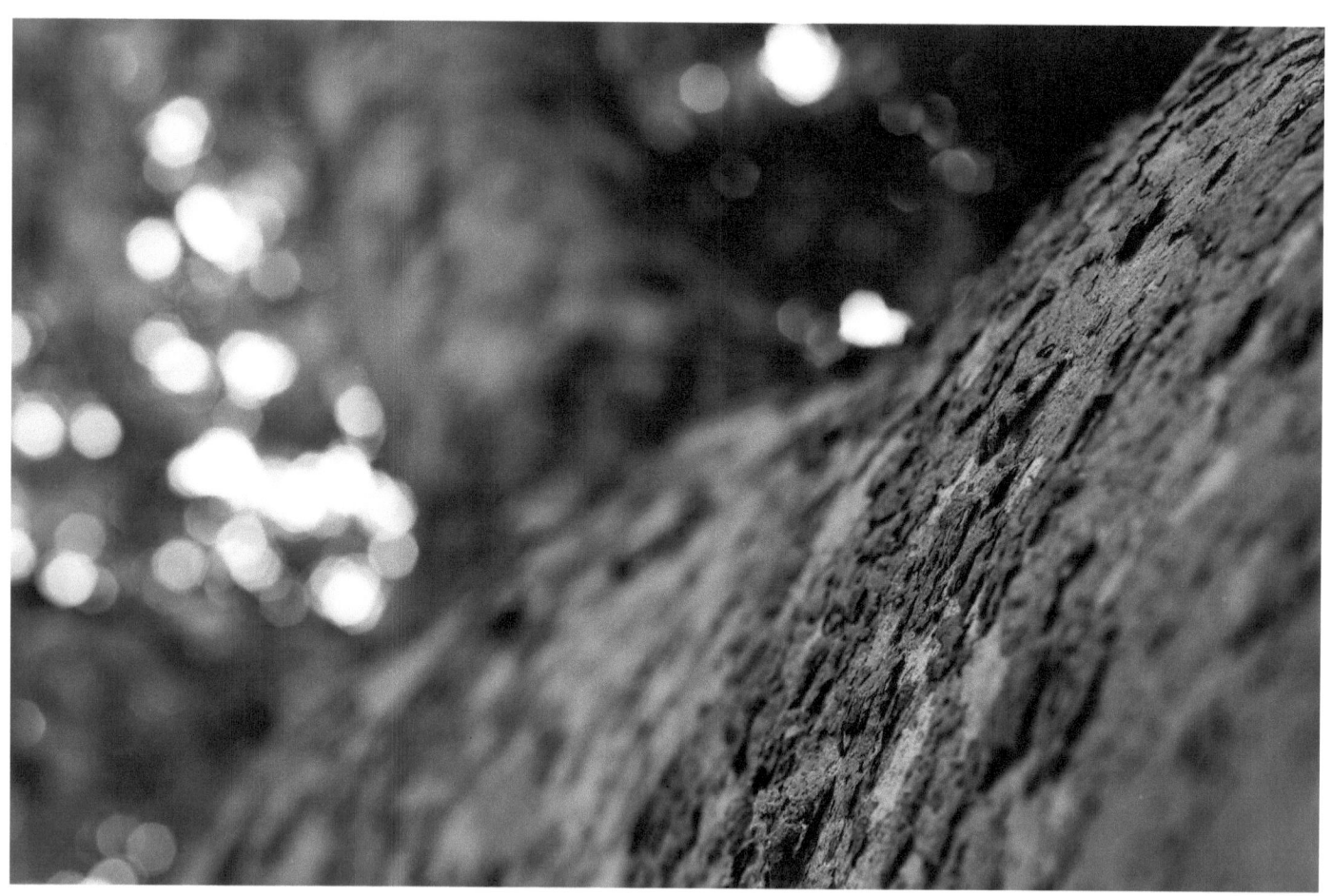

2068

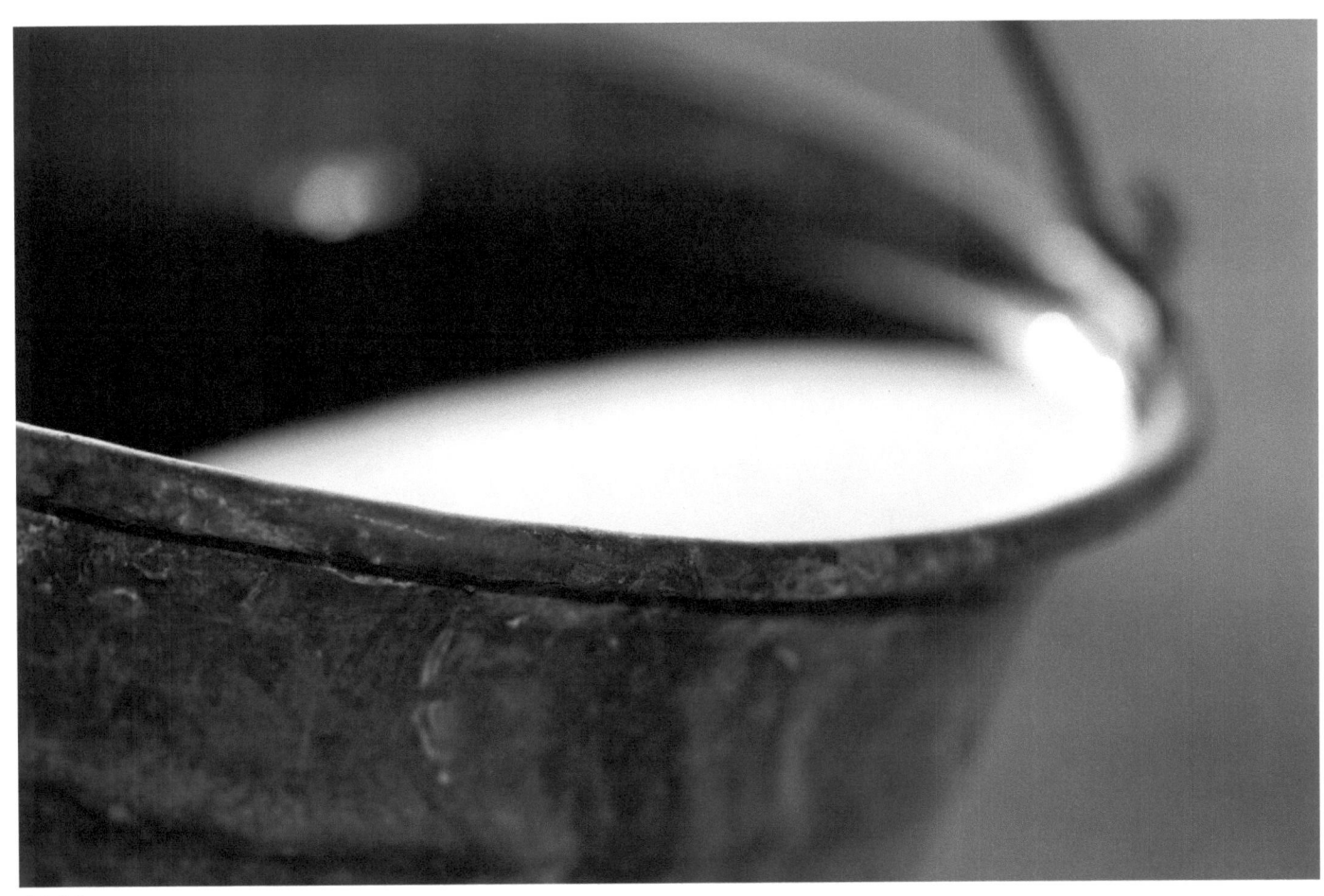

2180

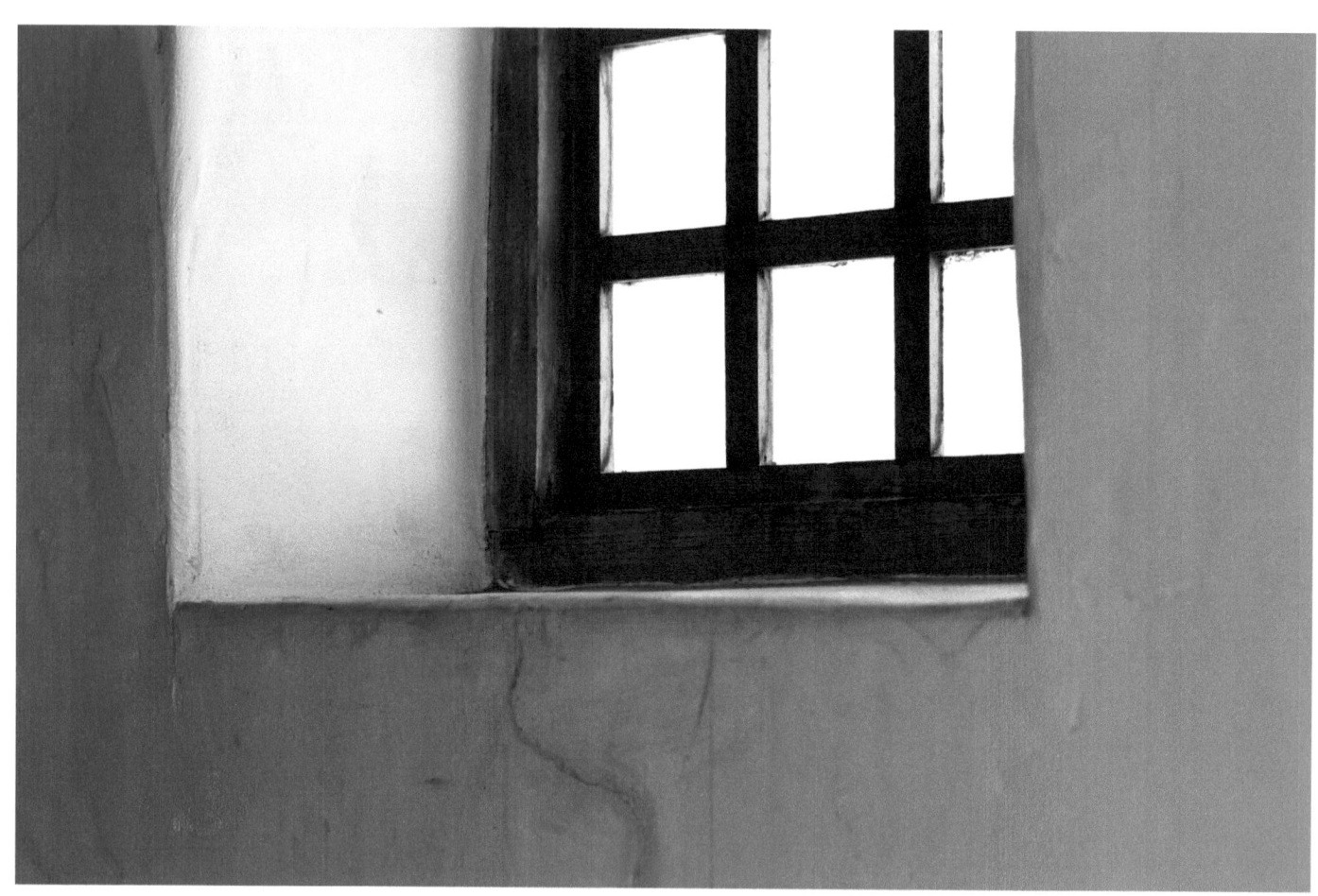

2397

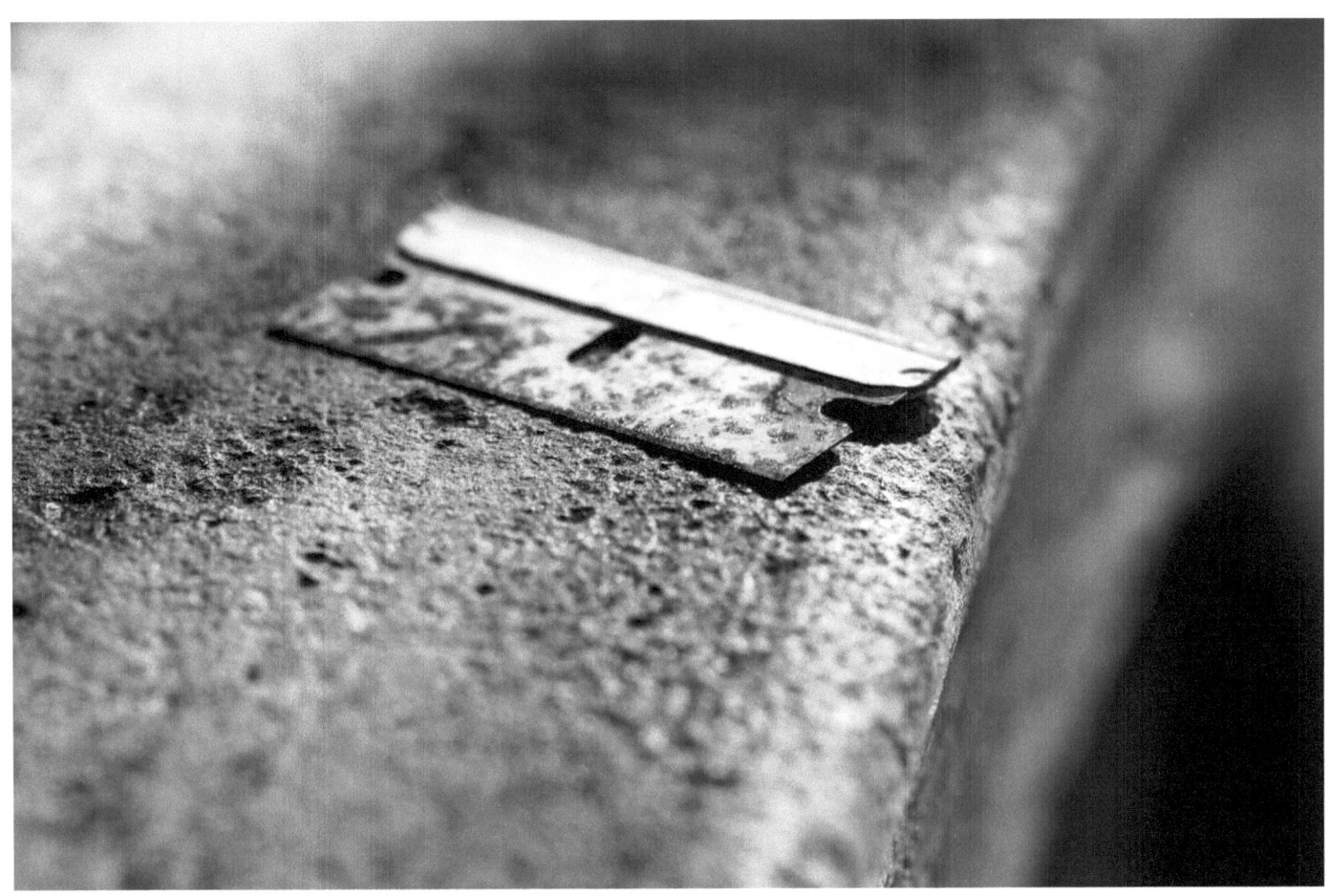

2467

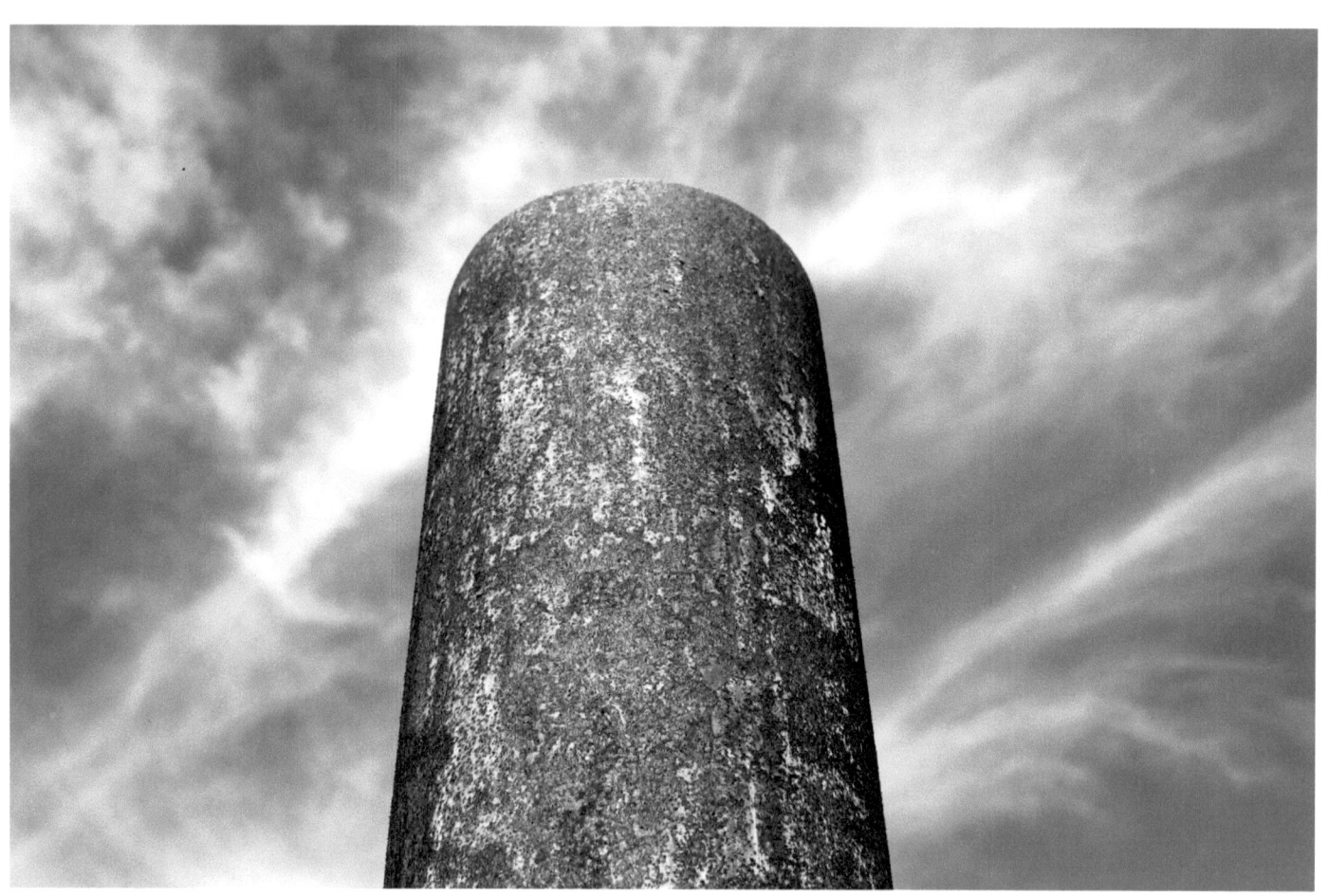

2495

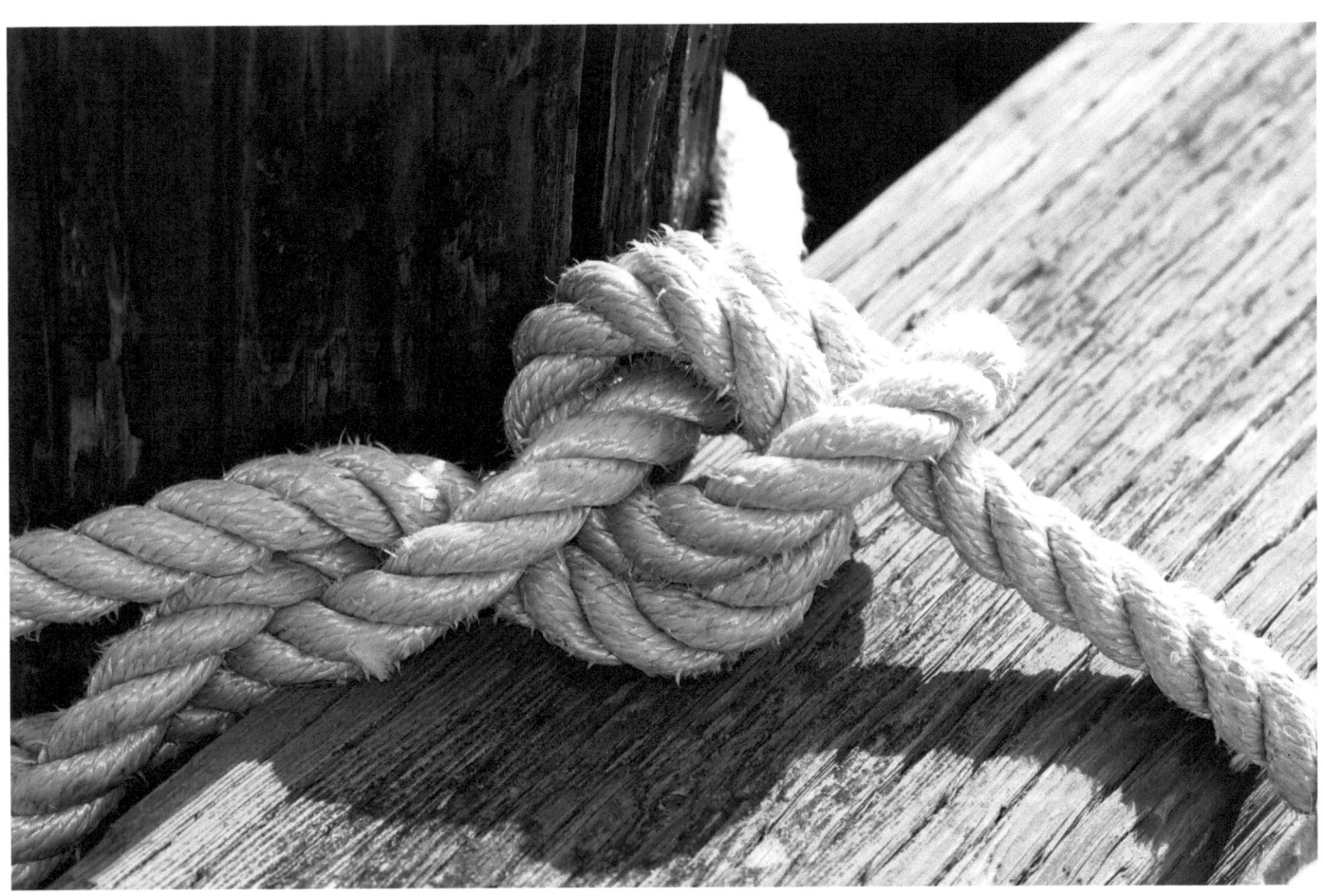

2631

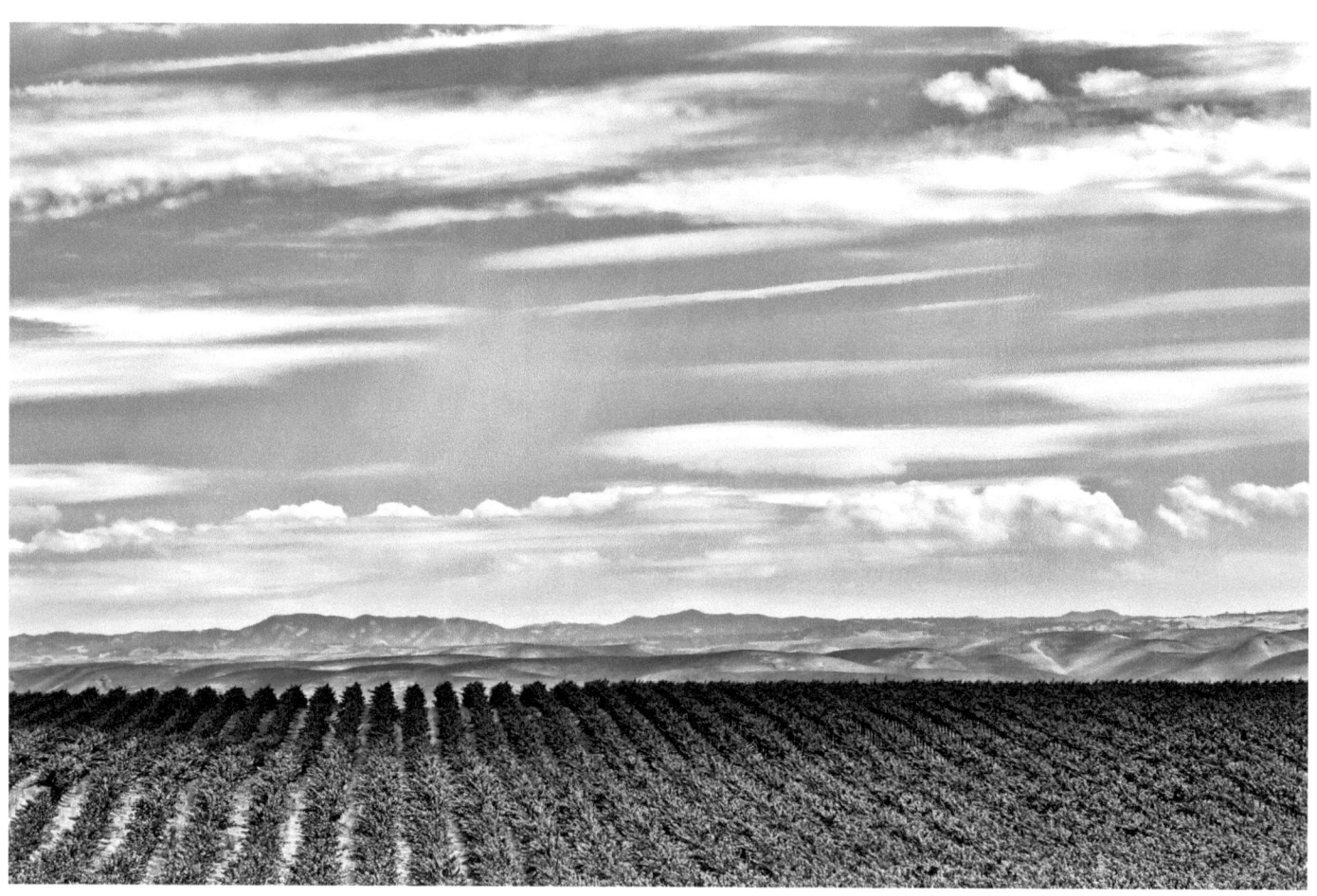

2929

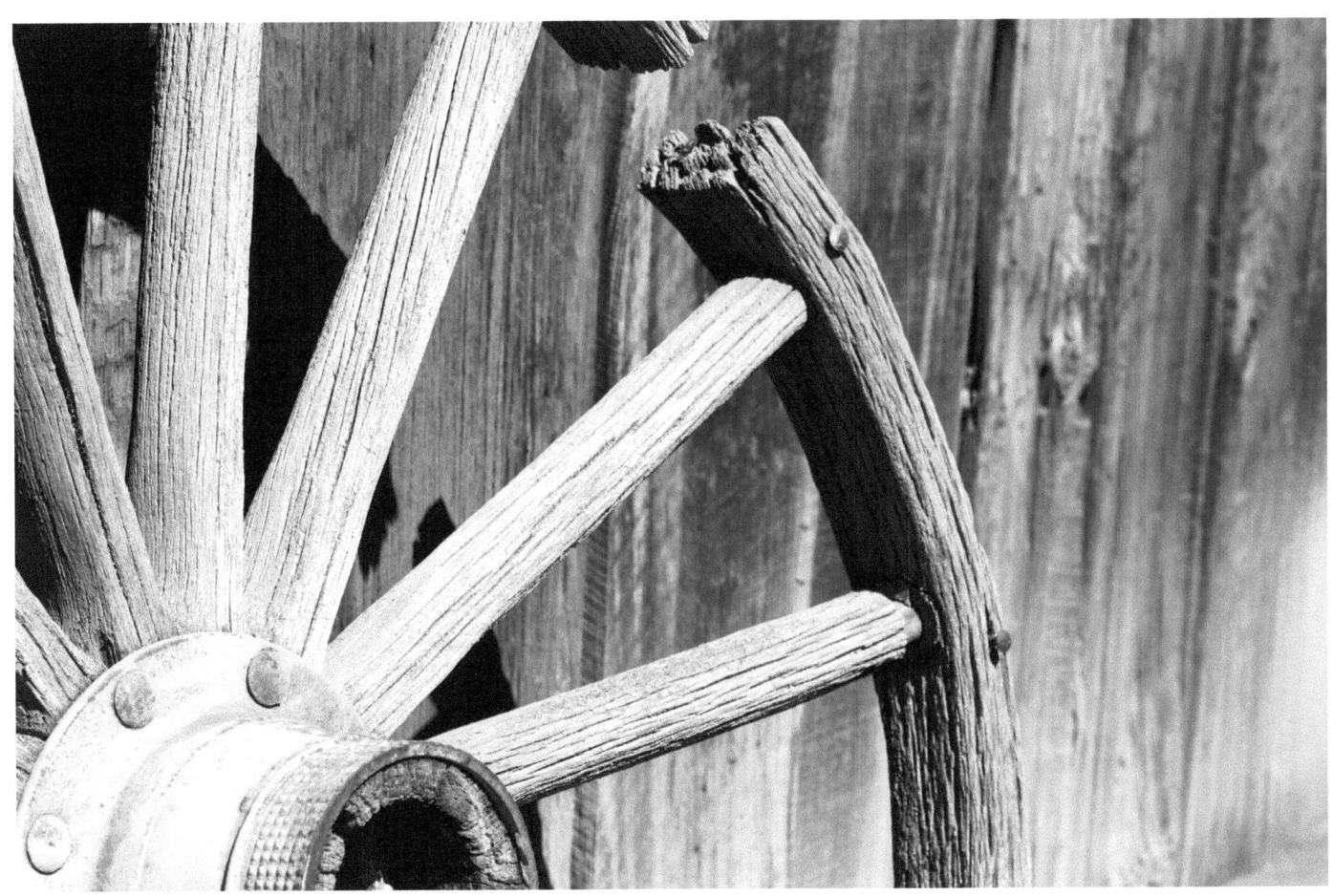

3147

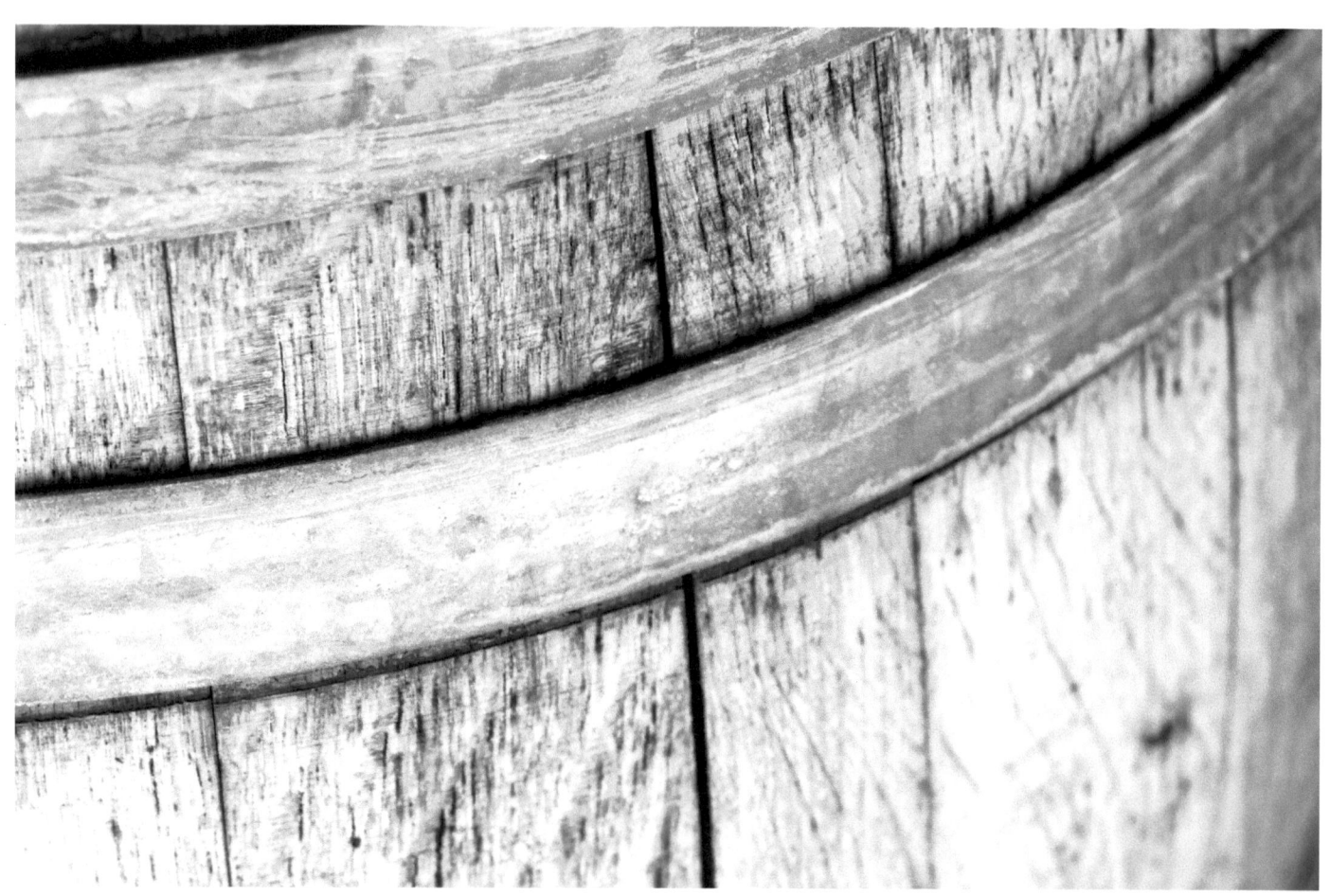

3151

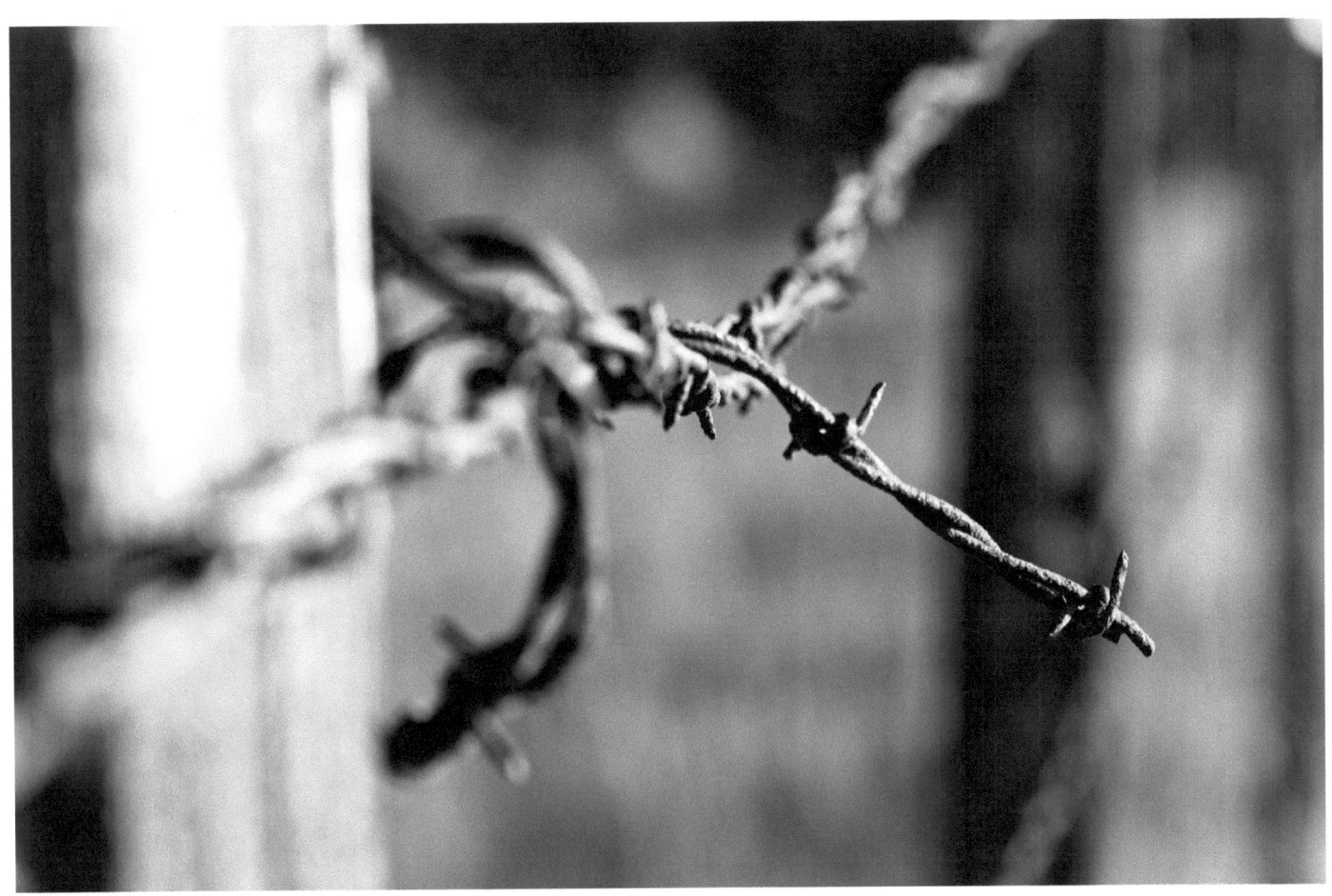

3359

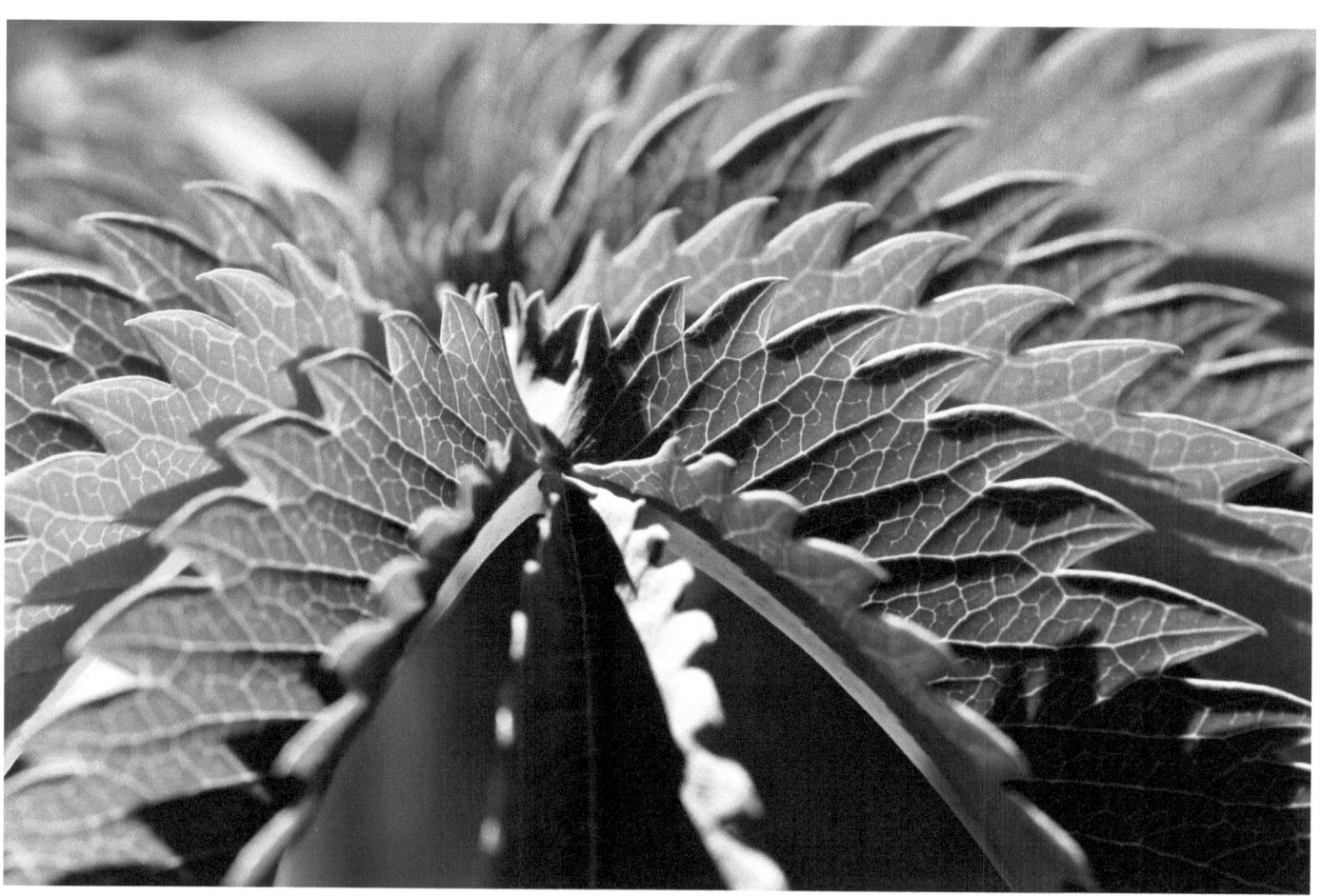

3714

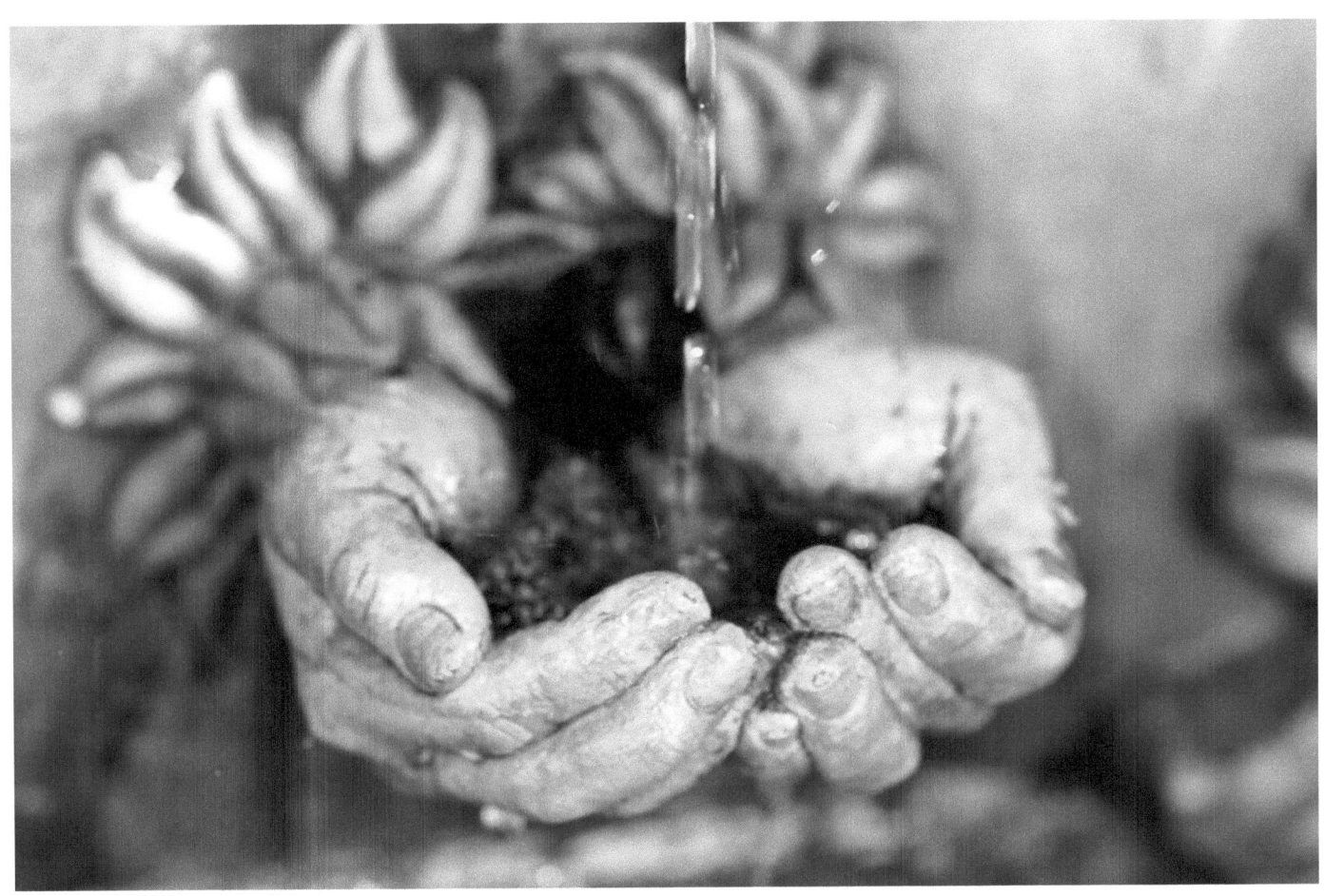

3720

3799

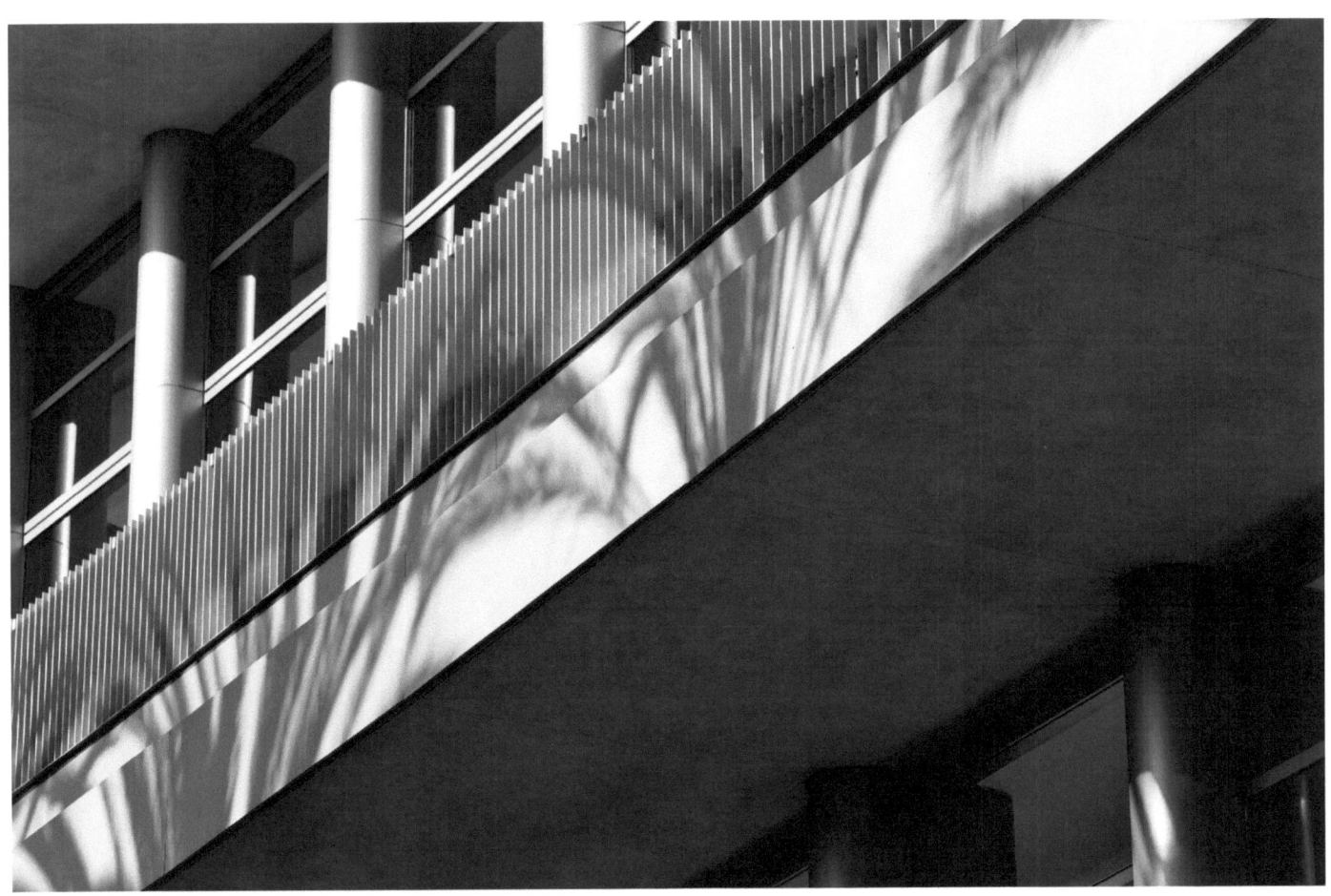

3916

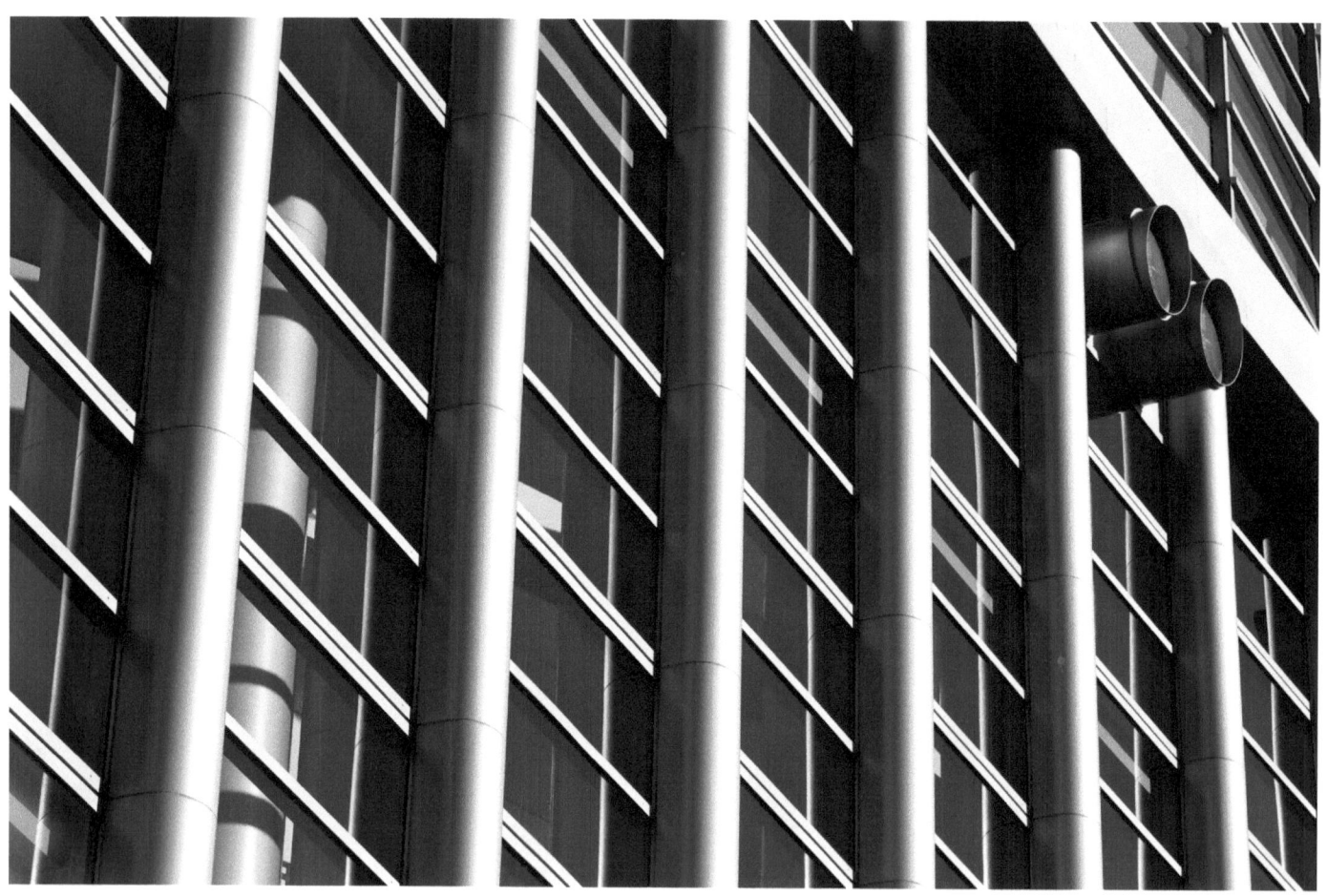

3943

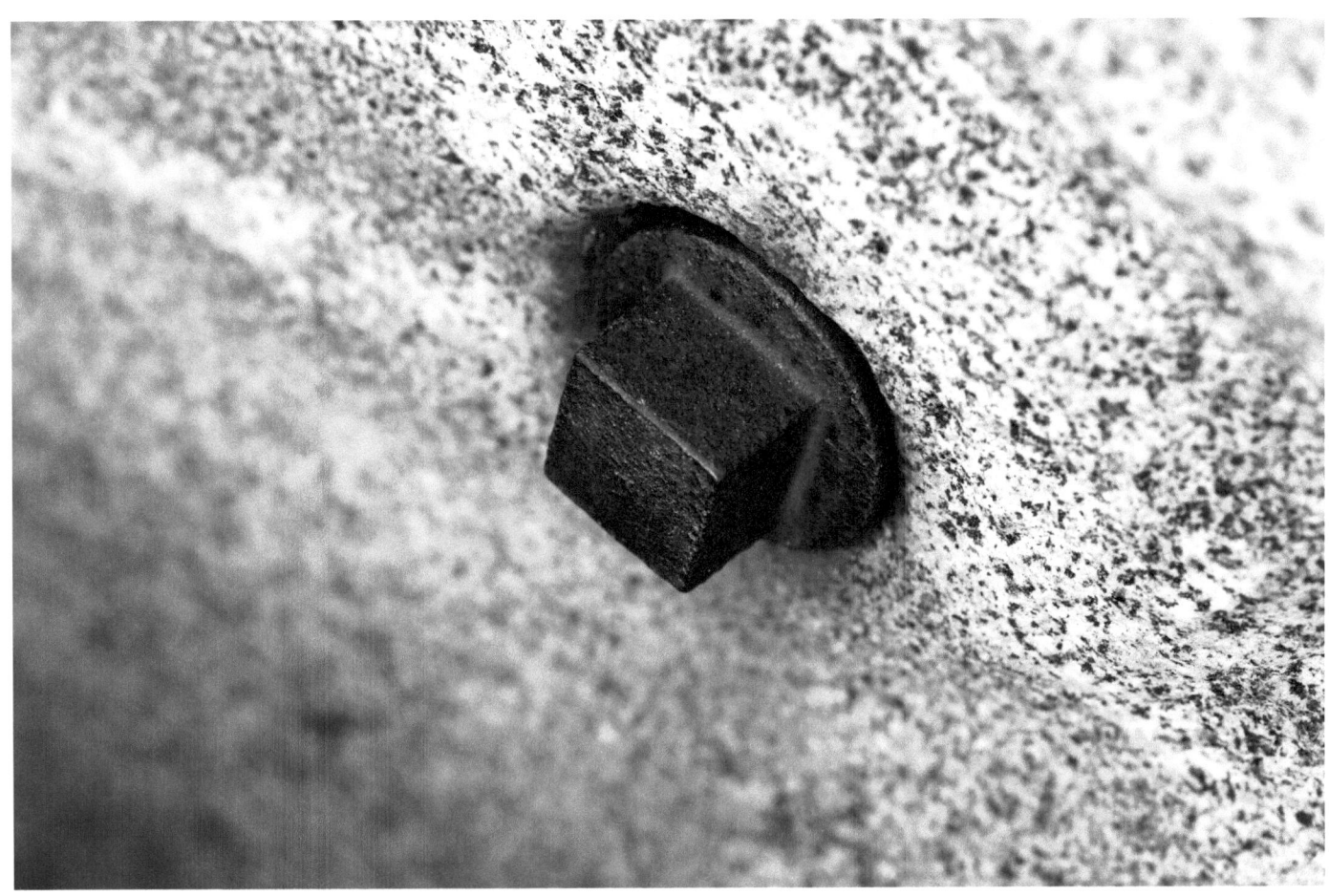

4035

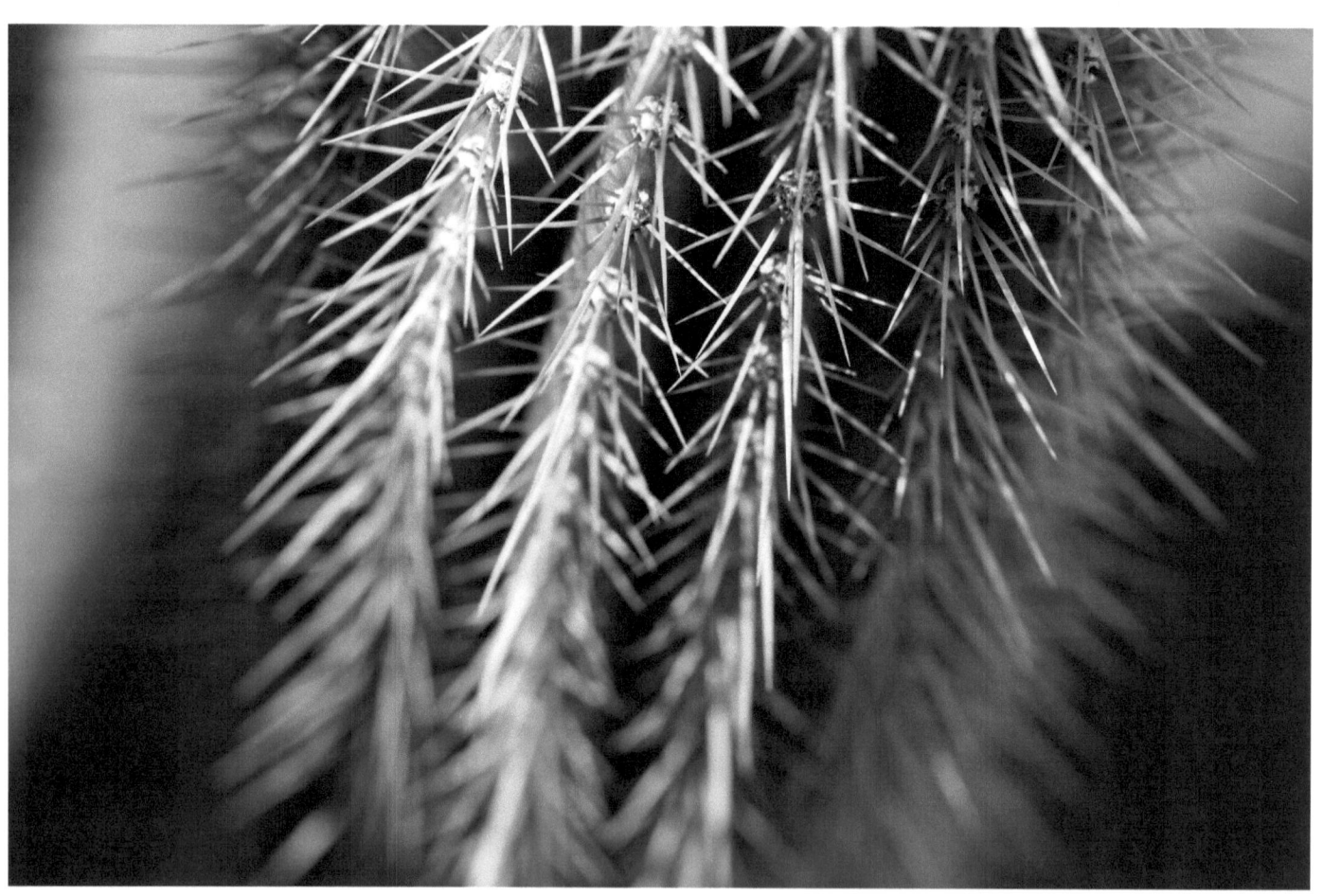

4070

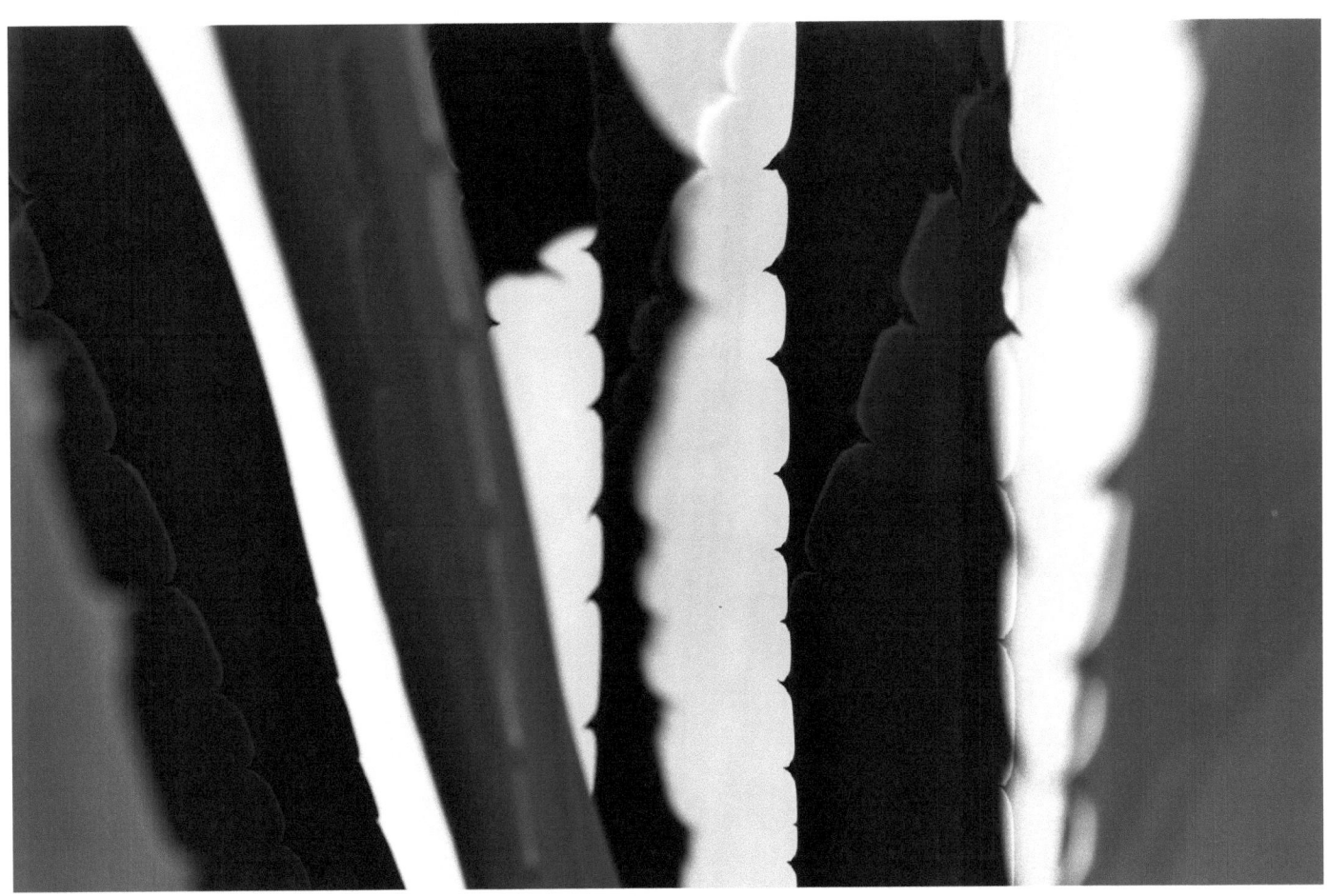

4099

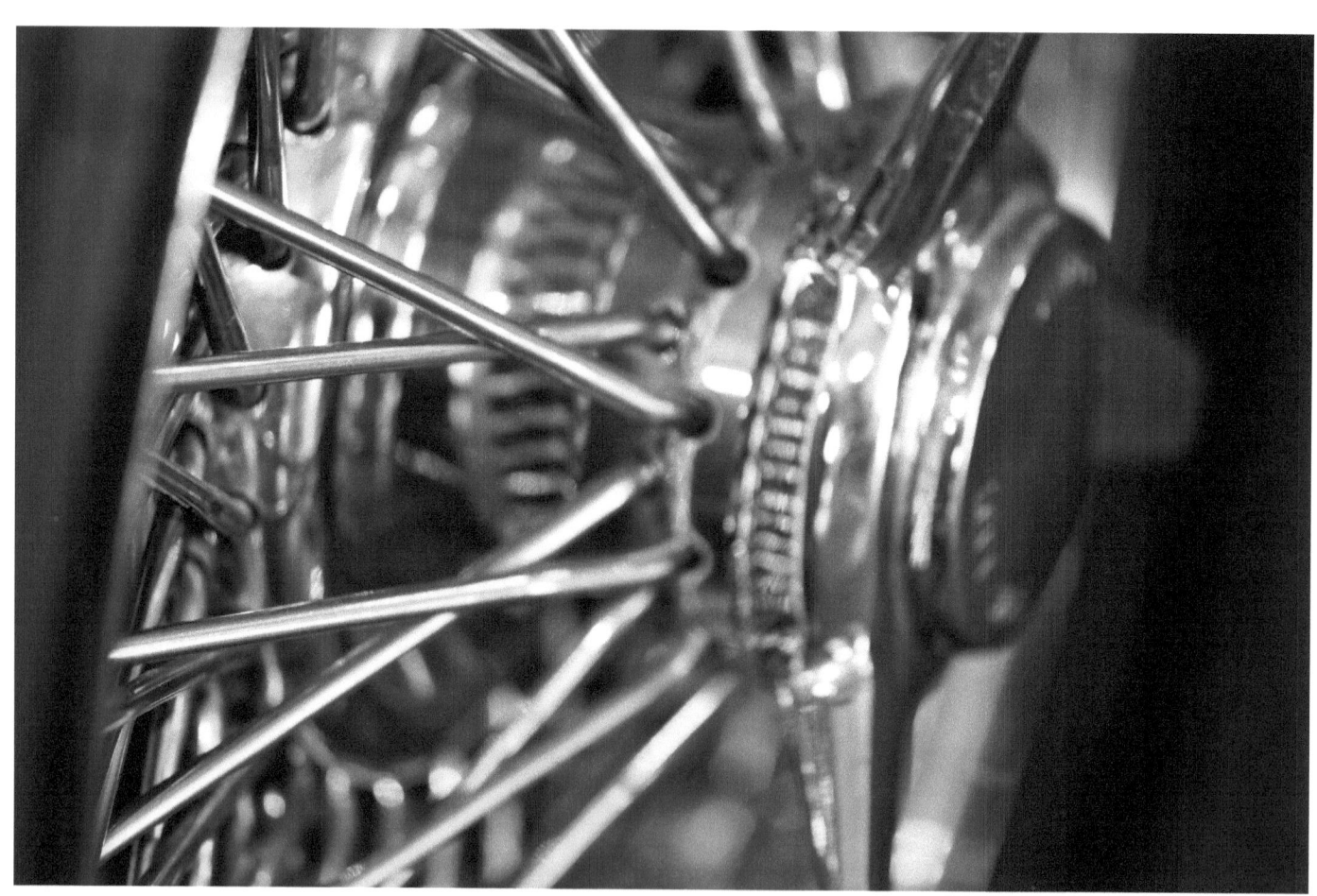

4193

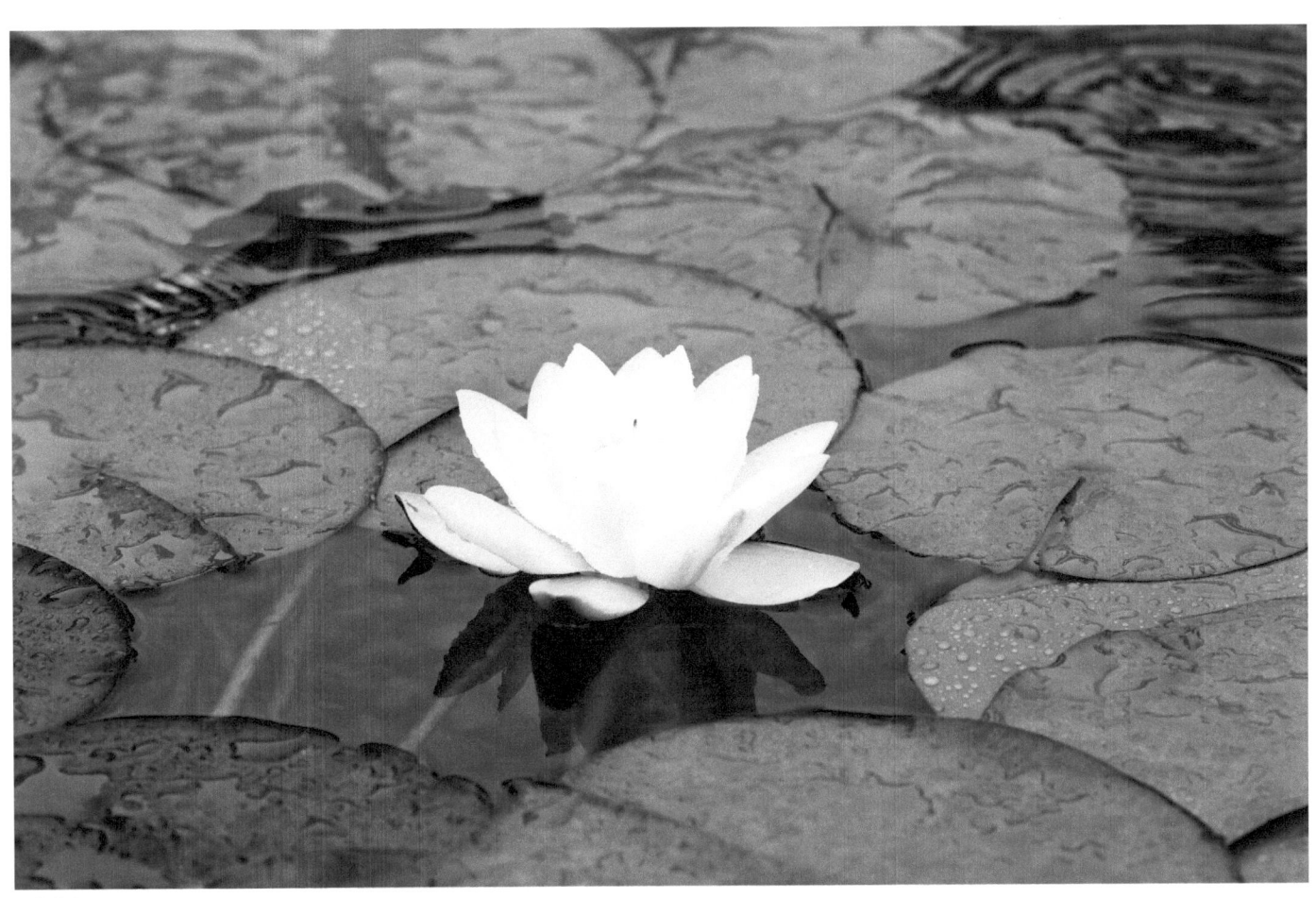

4265

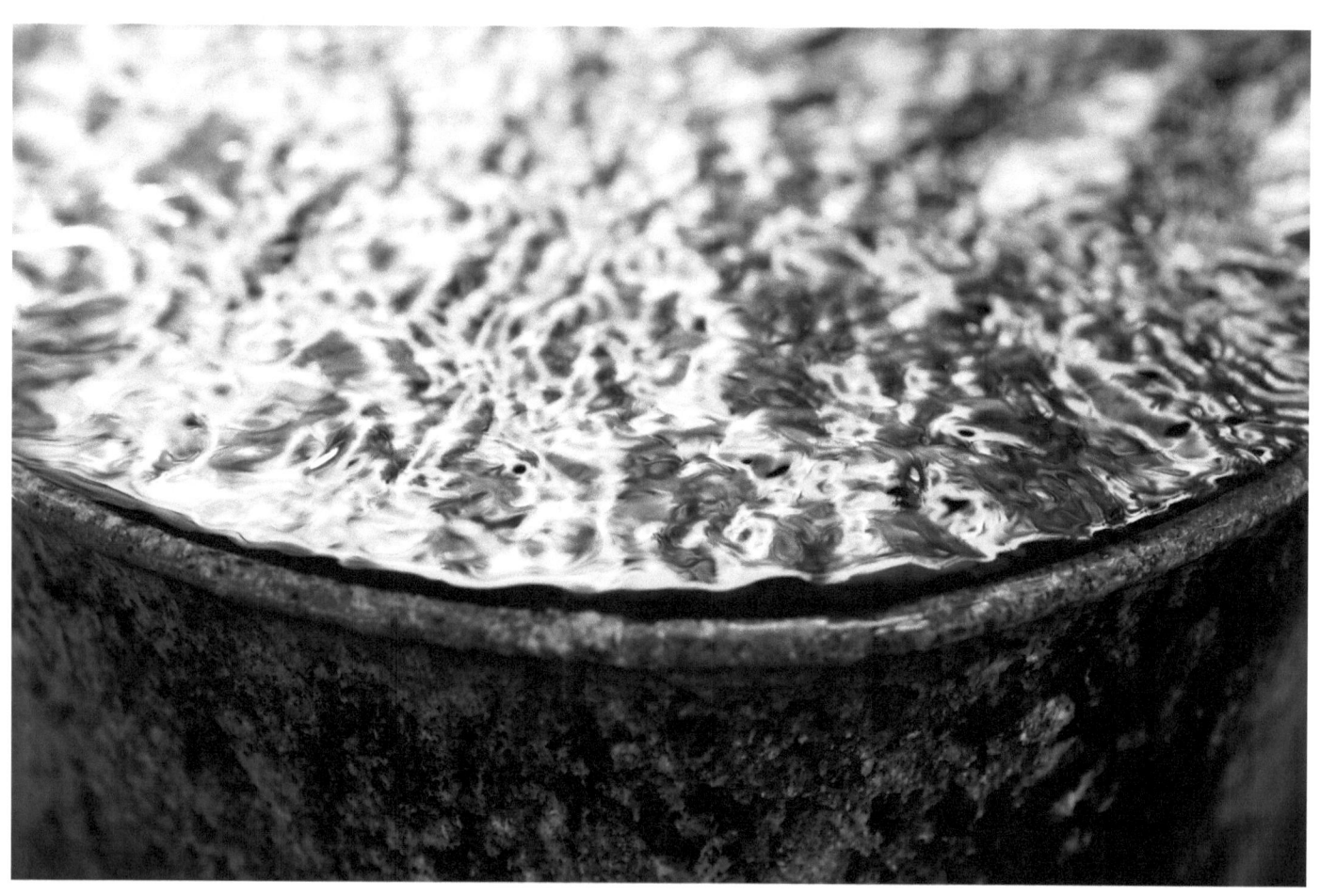

4533

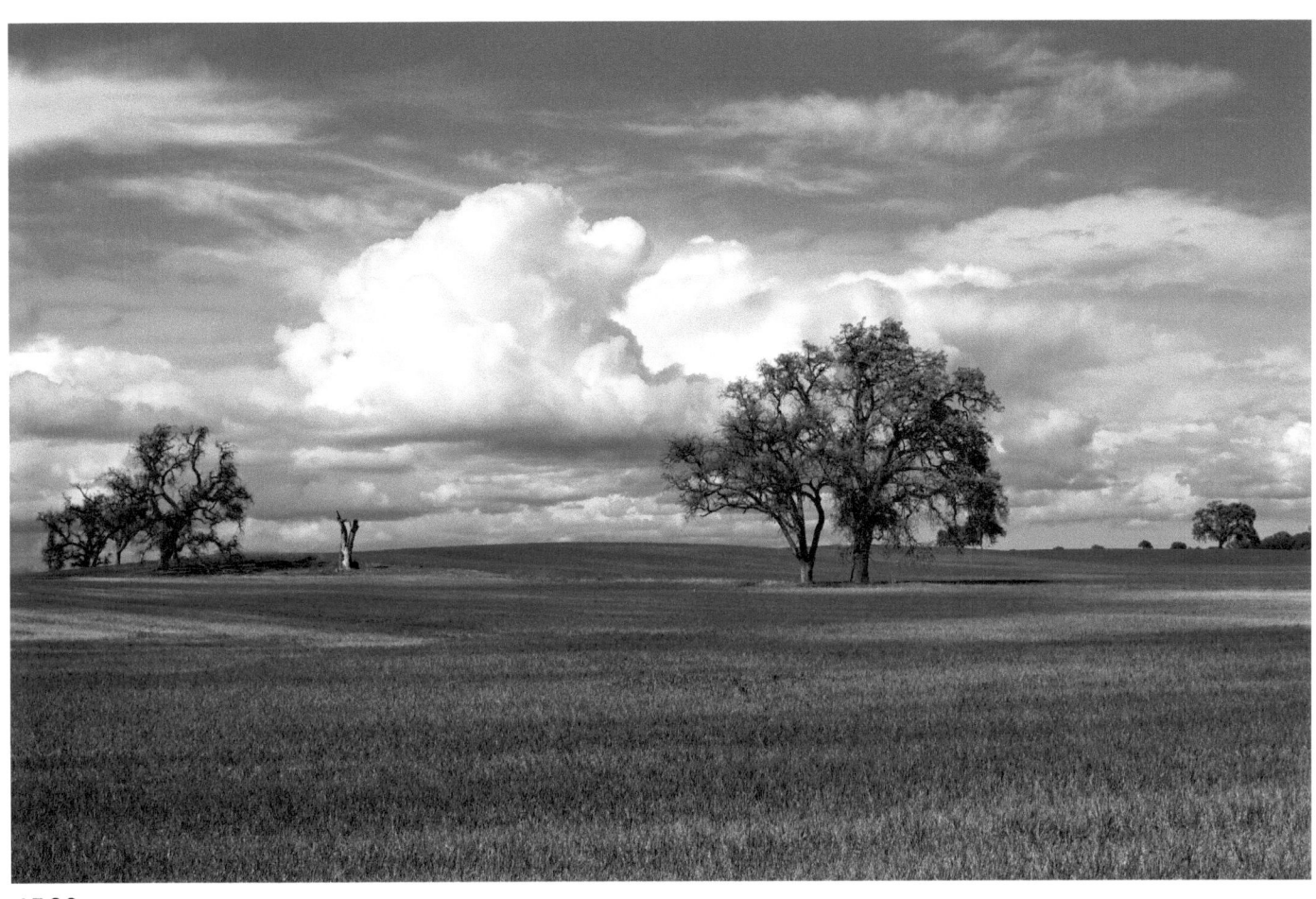

4560

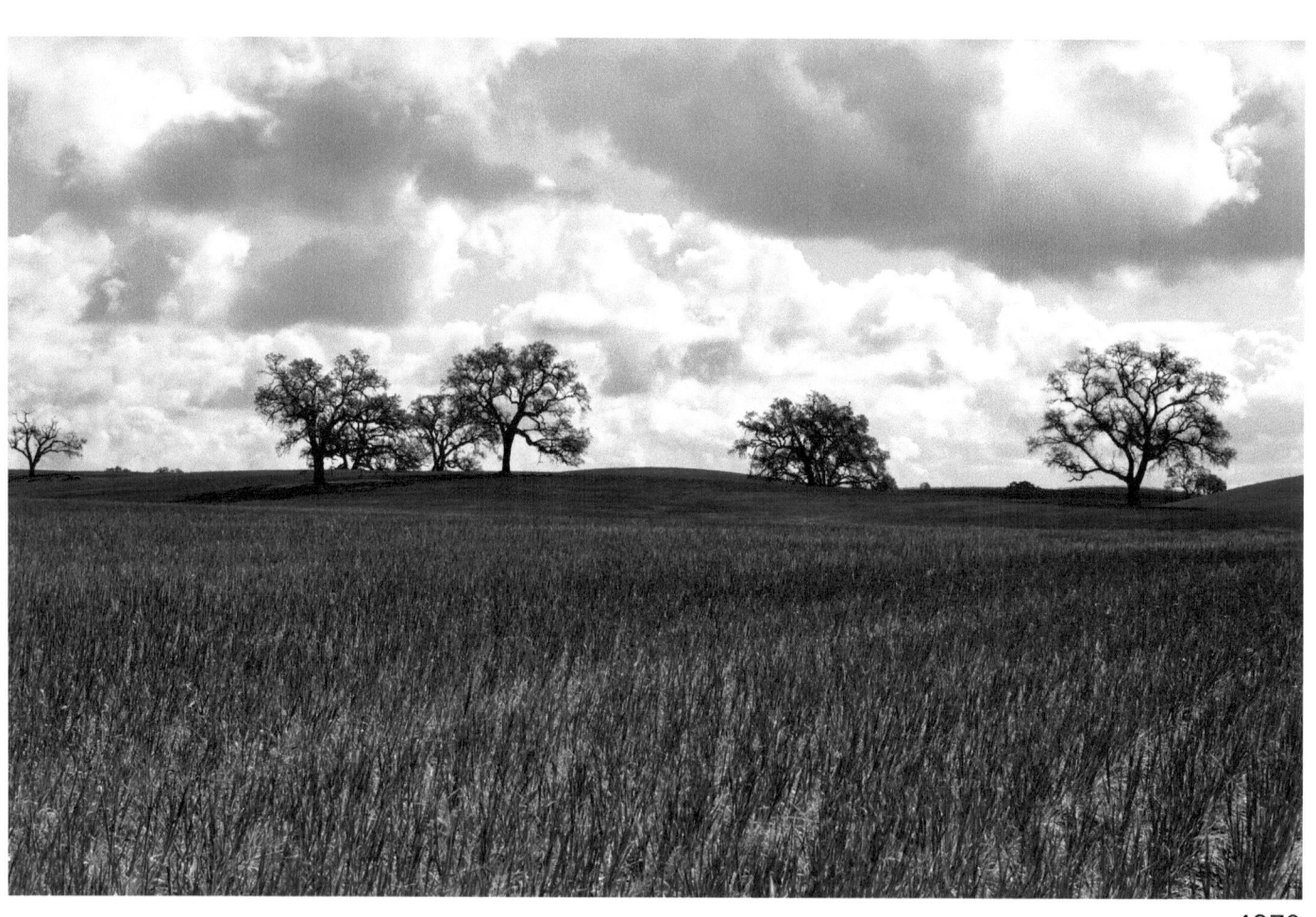

4879

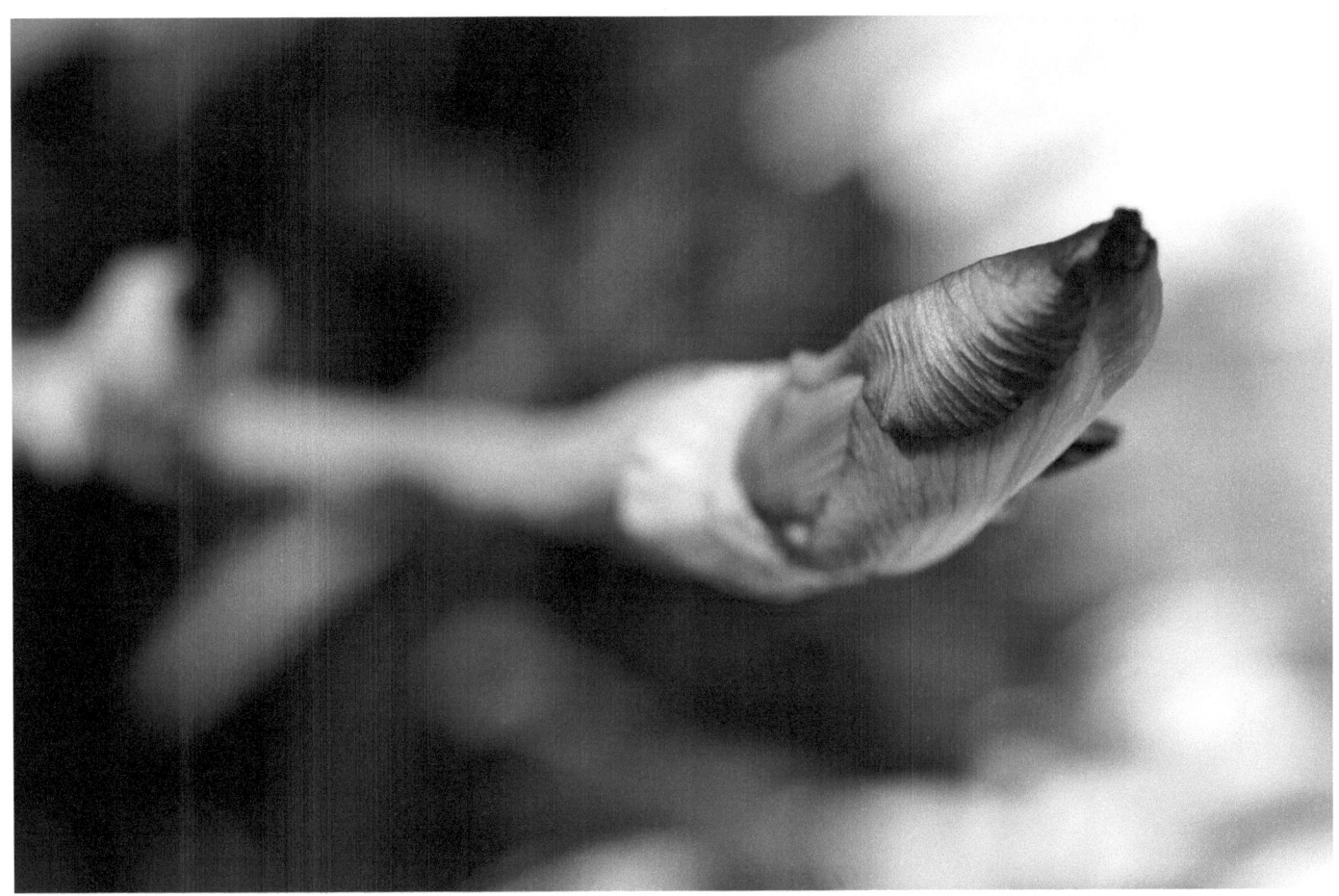

5492

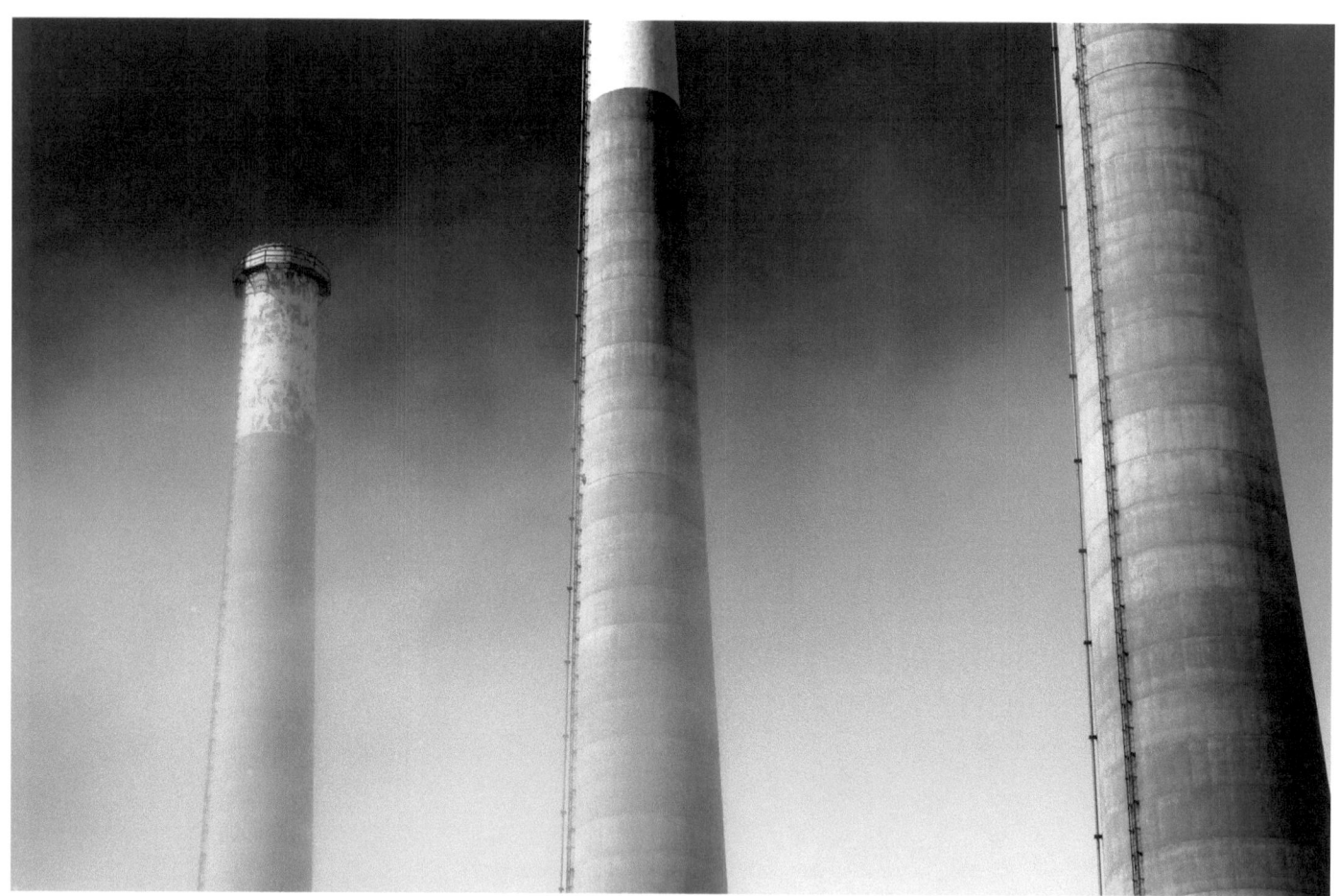

5541

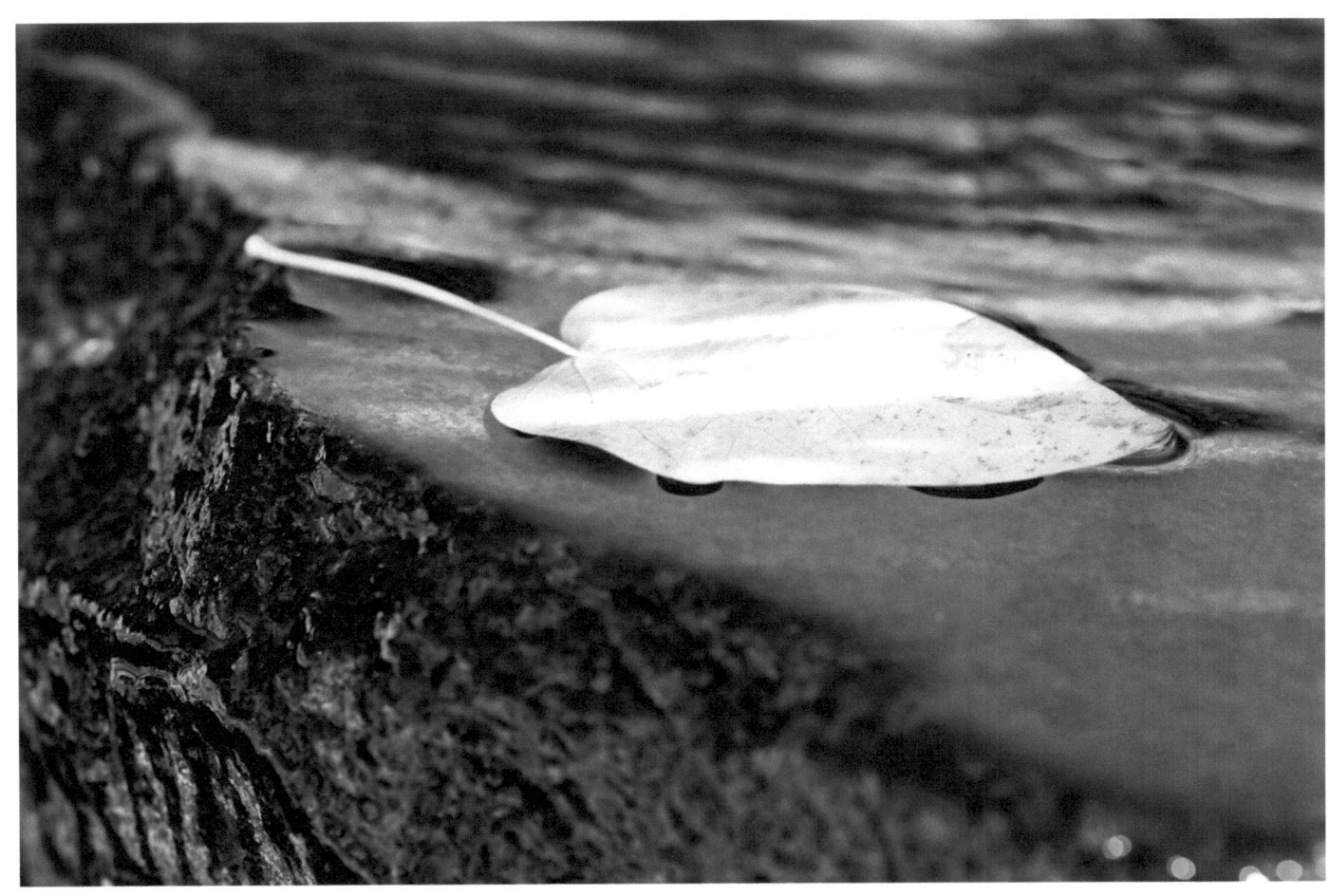

5750

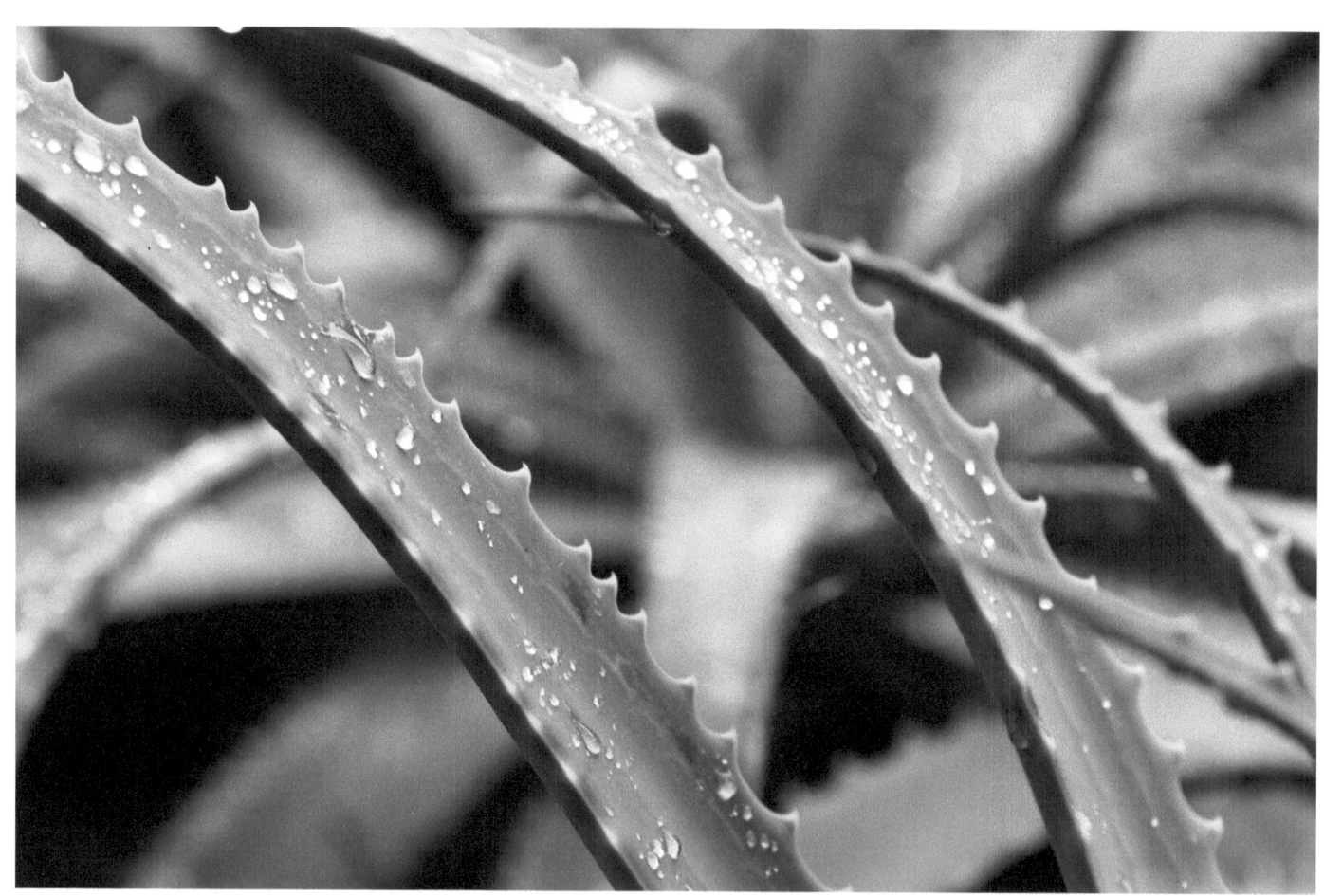

5784

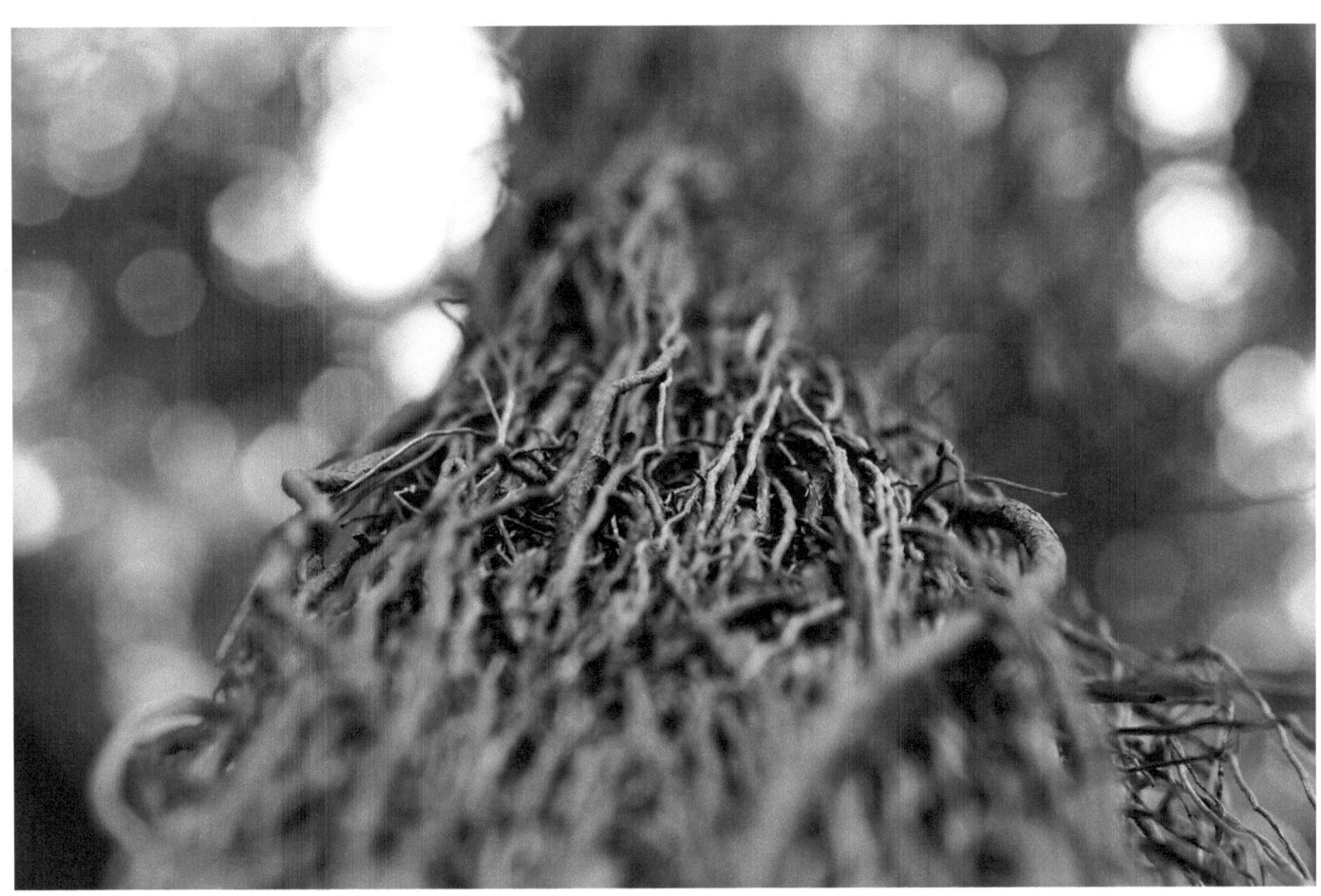

5811

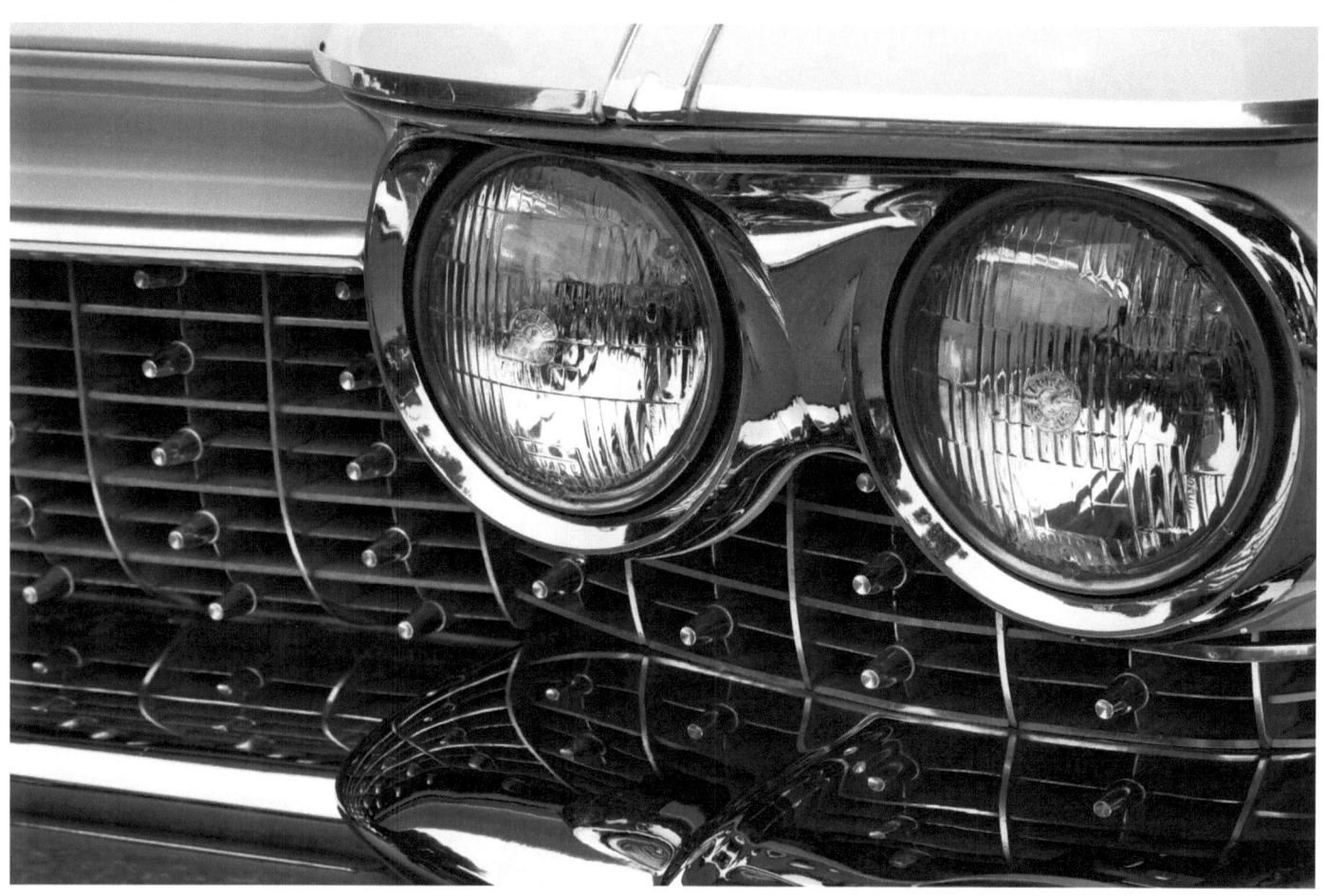

5844

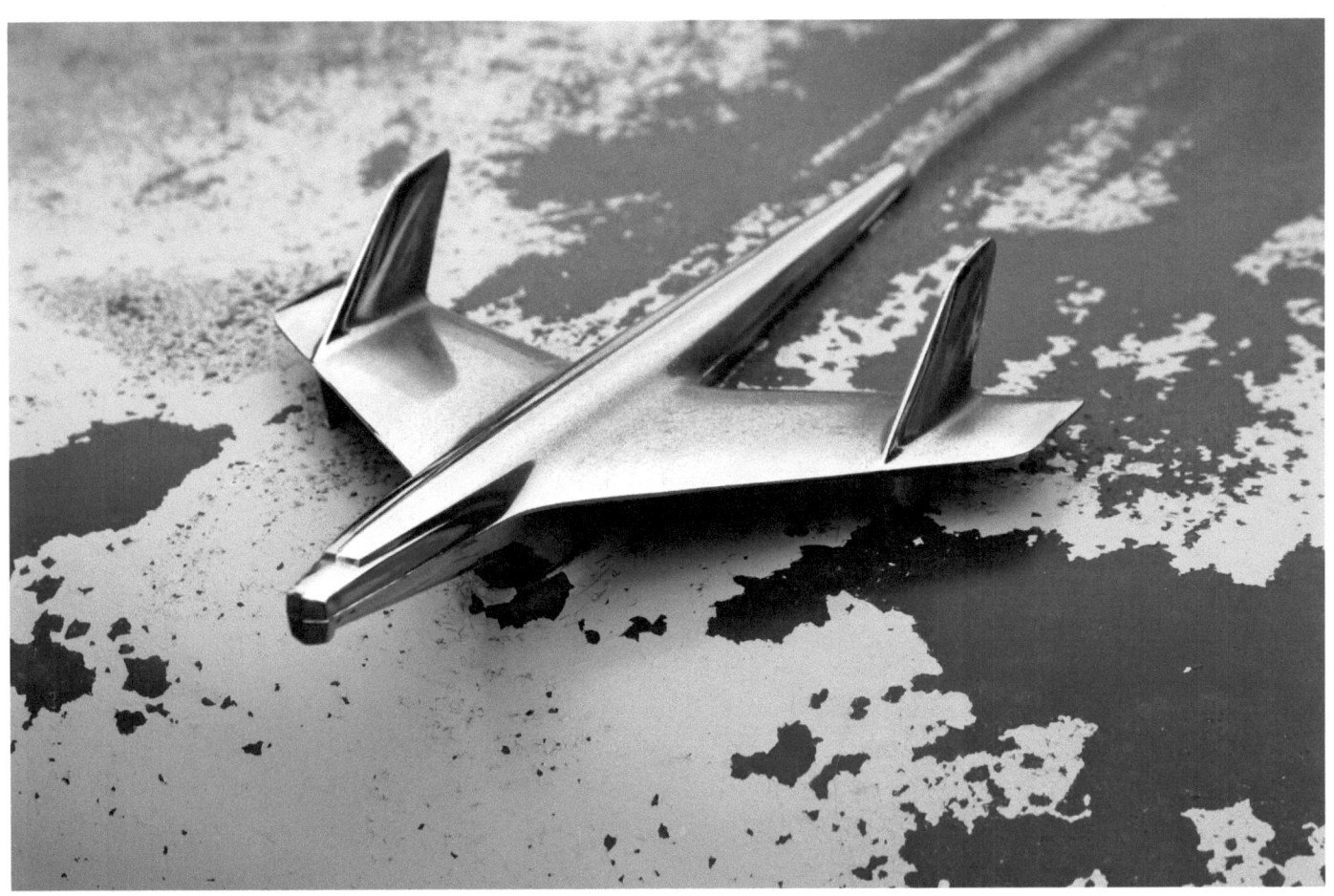

5846

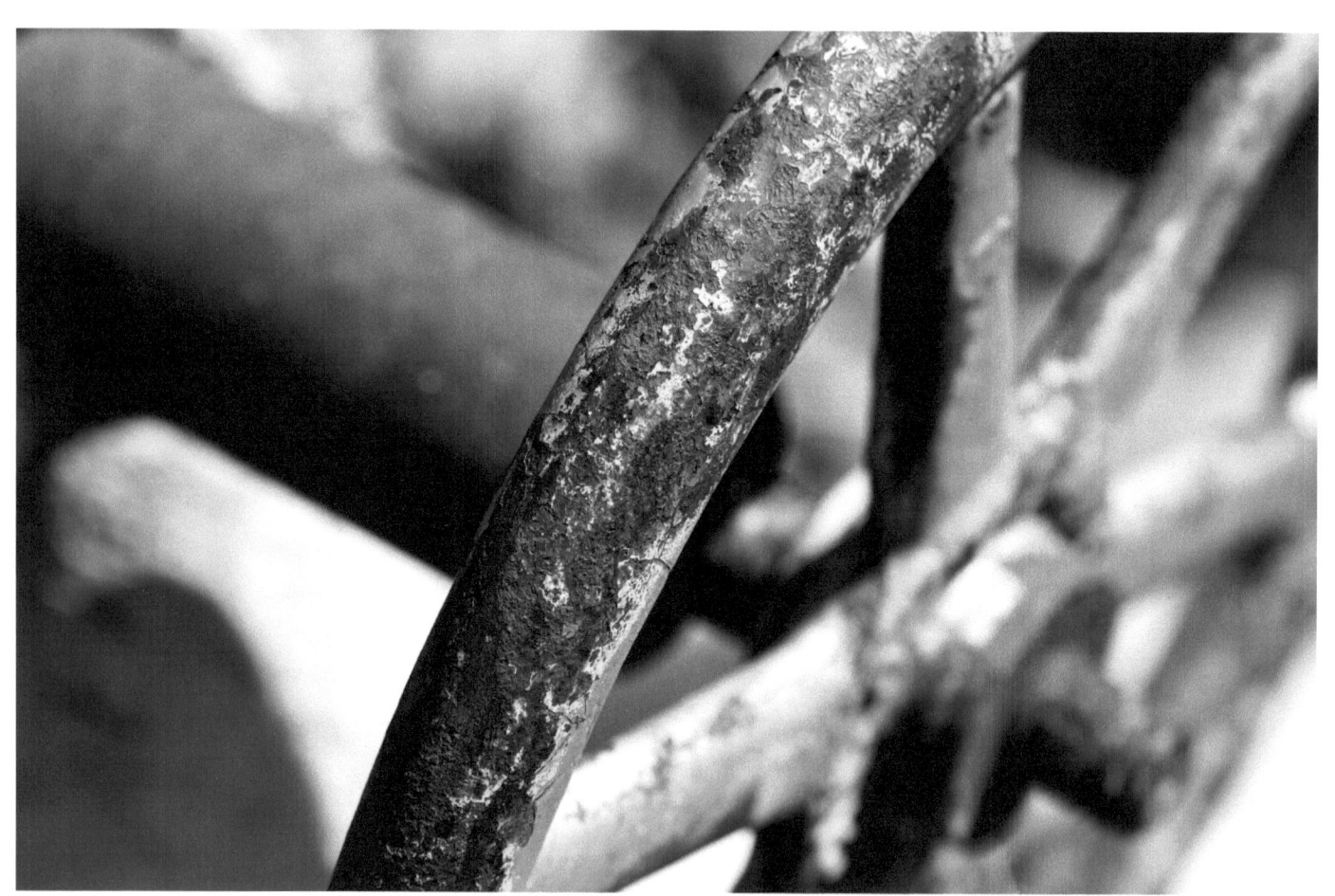

6095

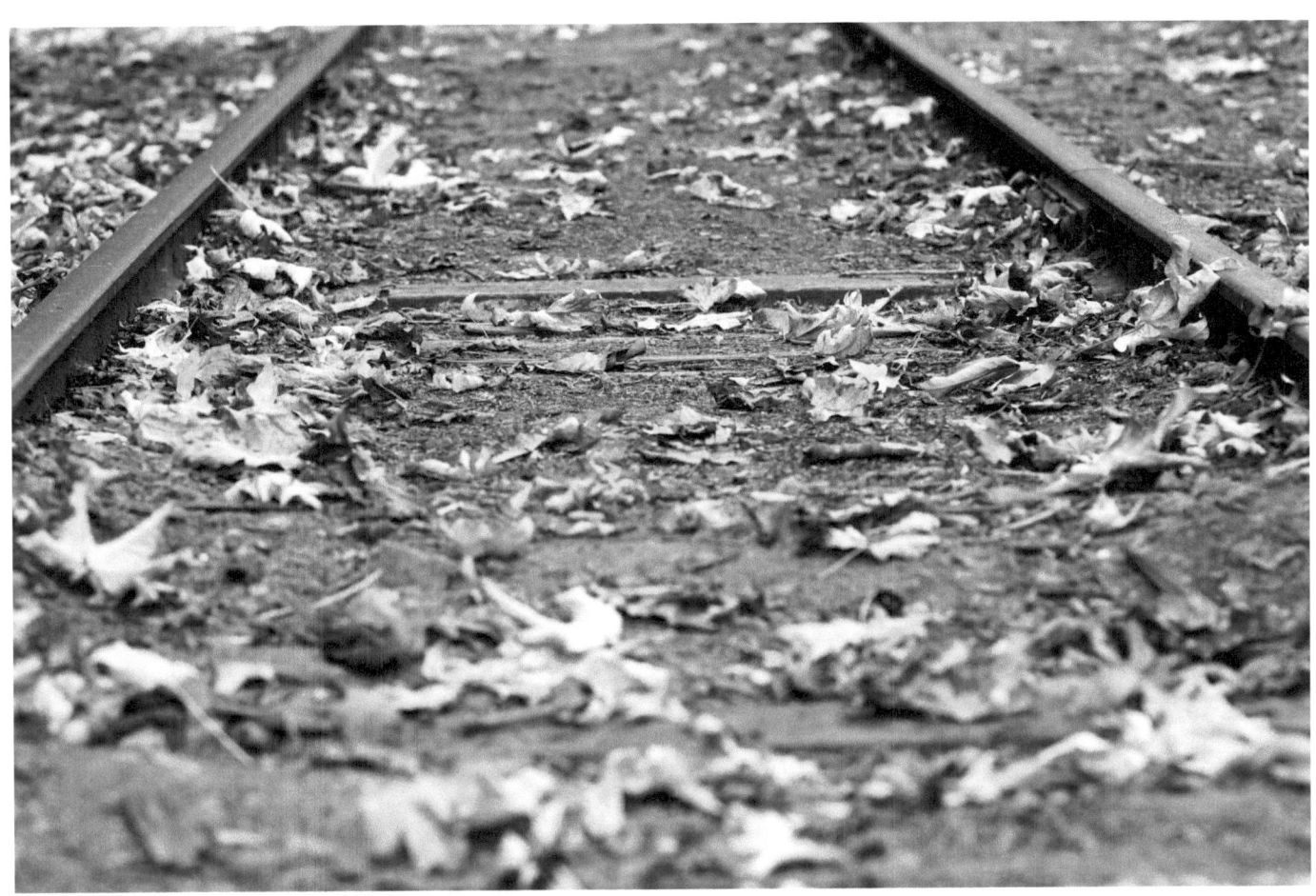

6176

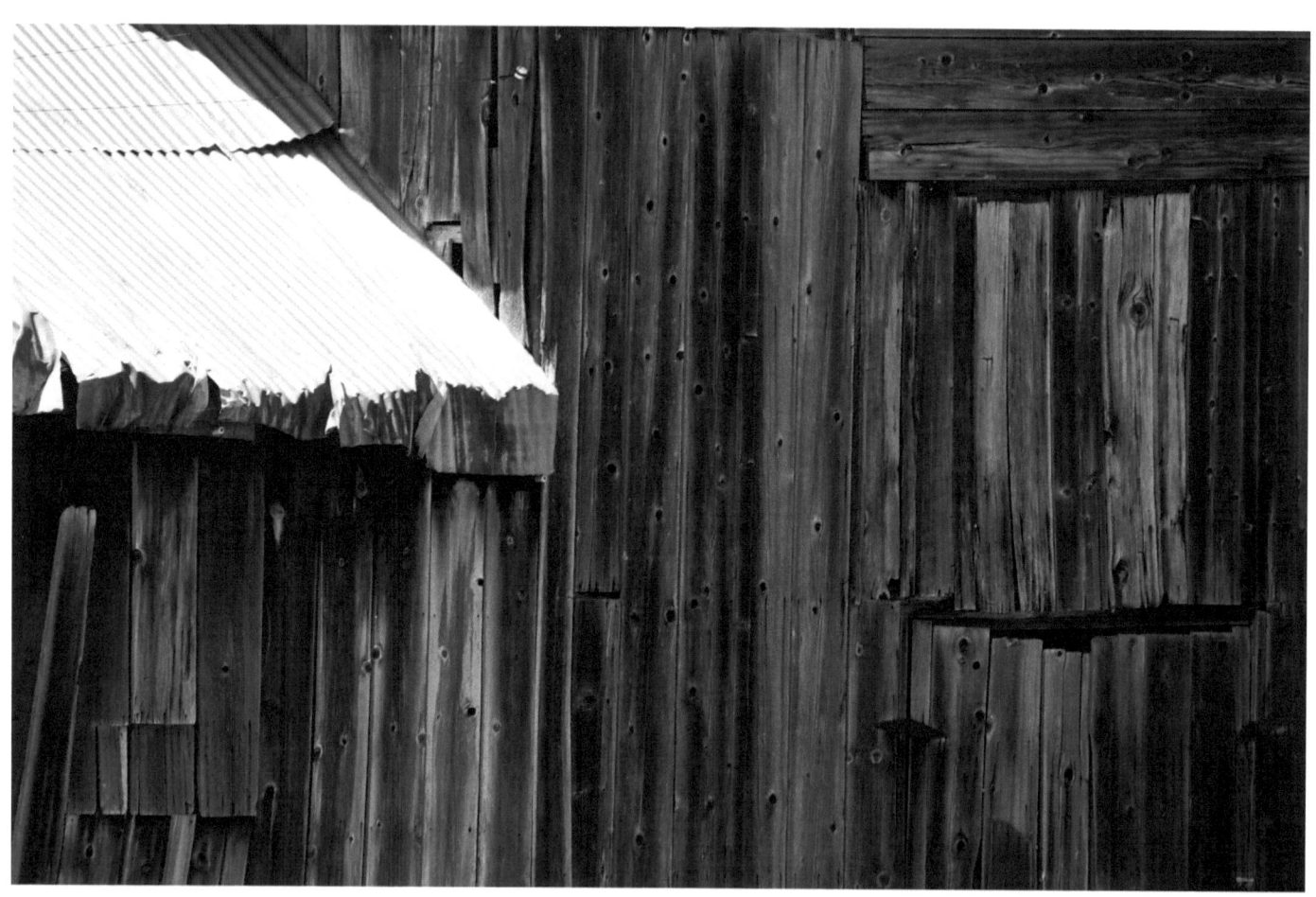

6946

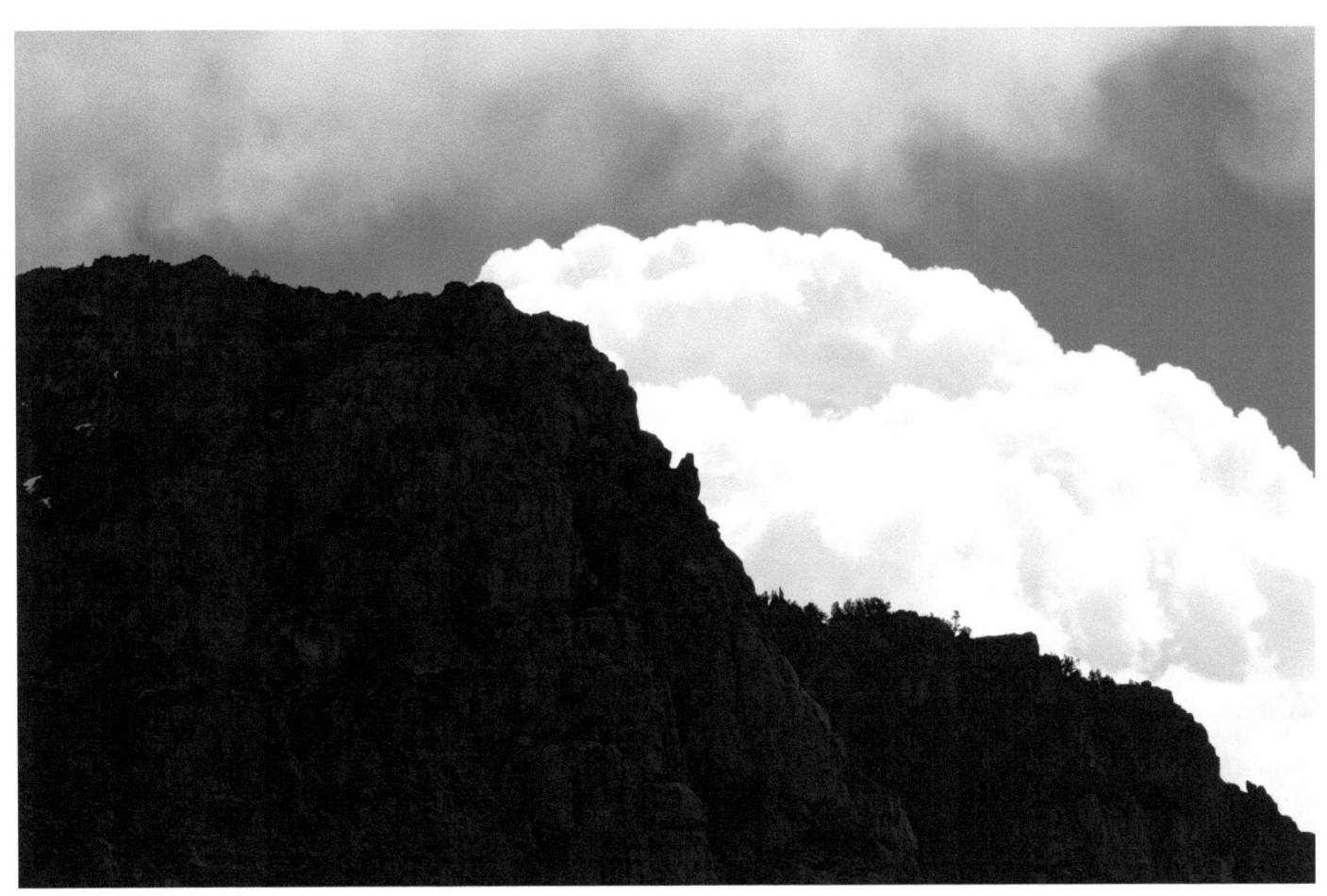

7148

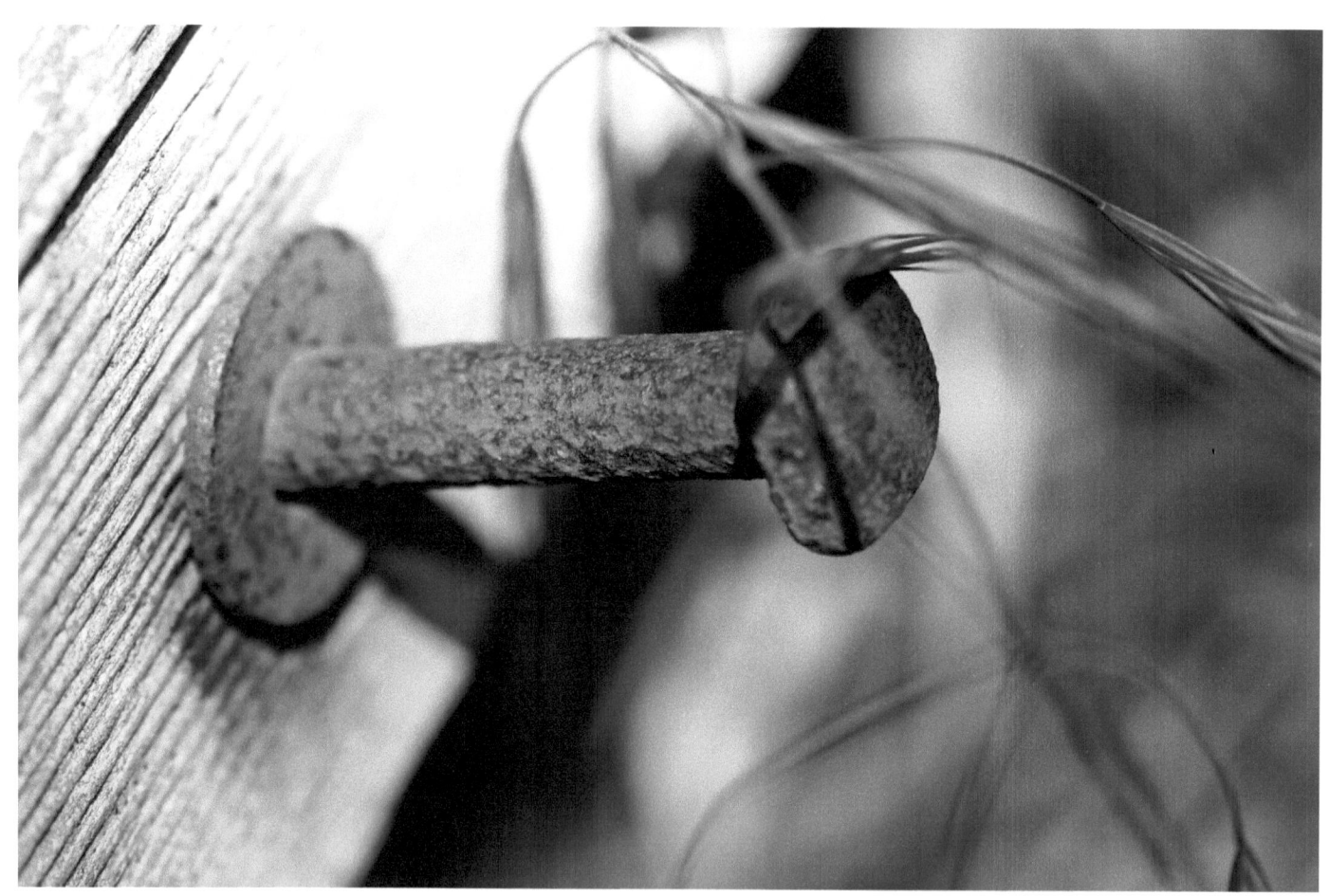

7182

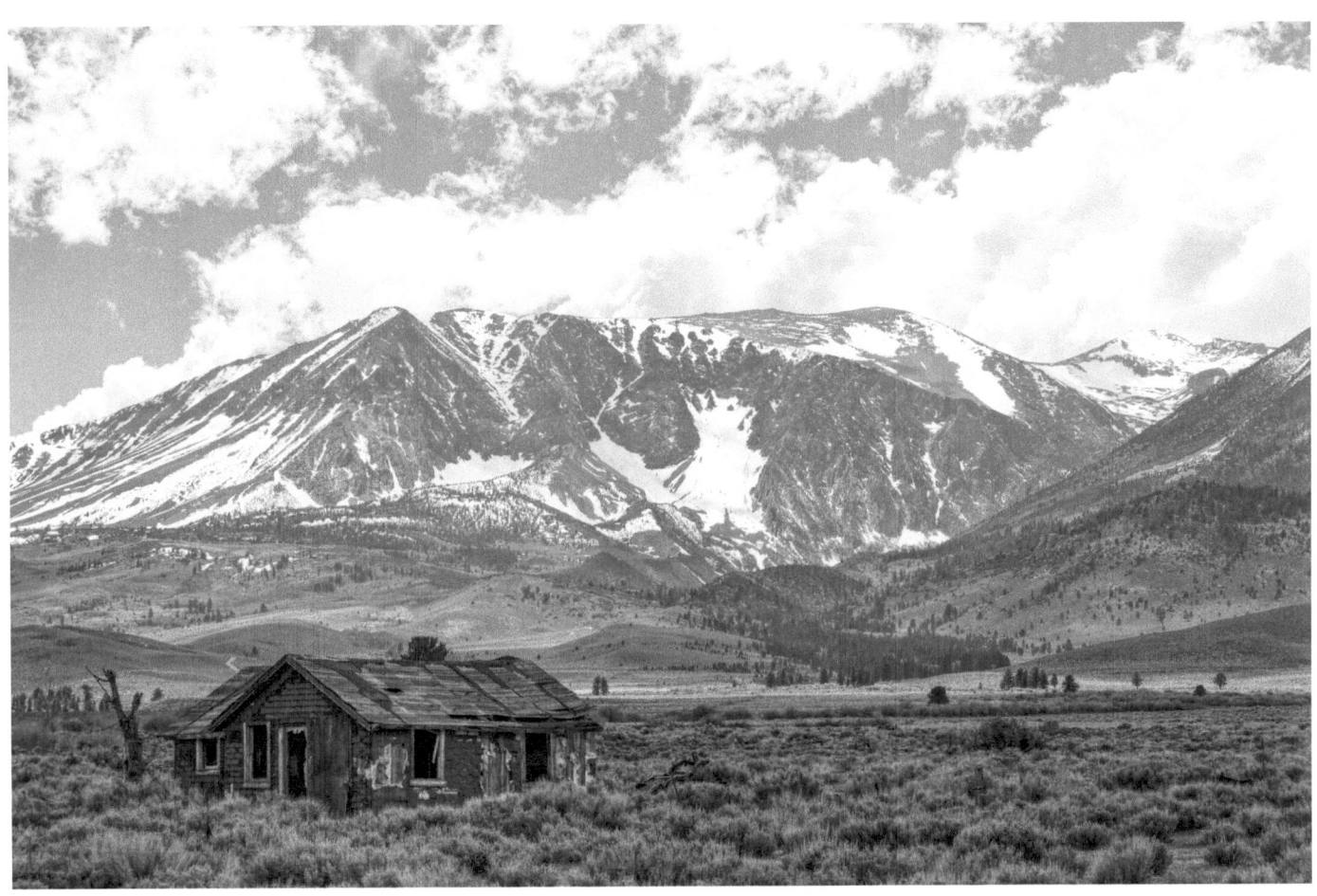

7339

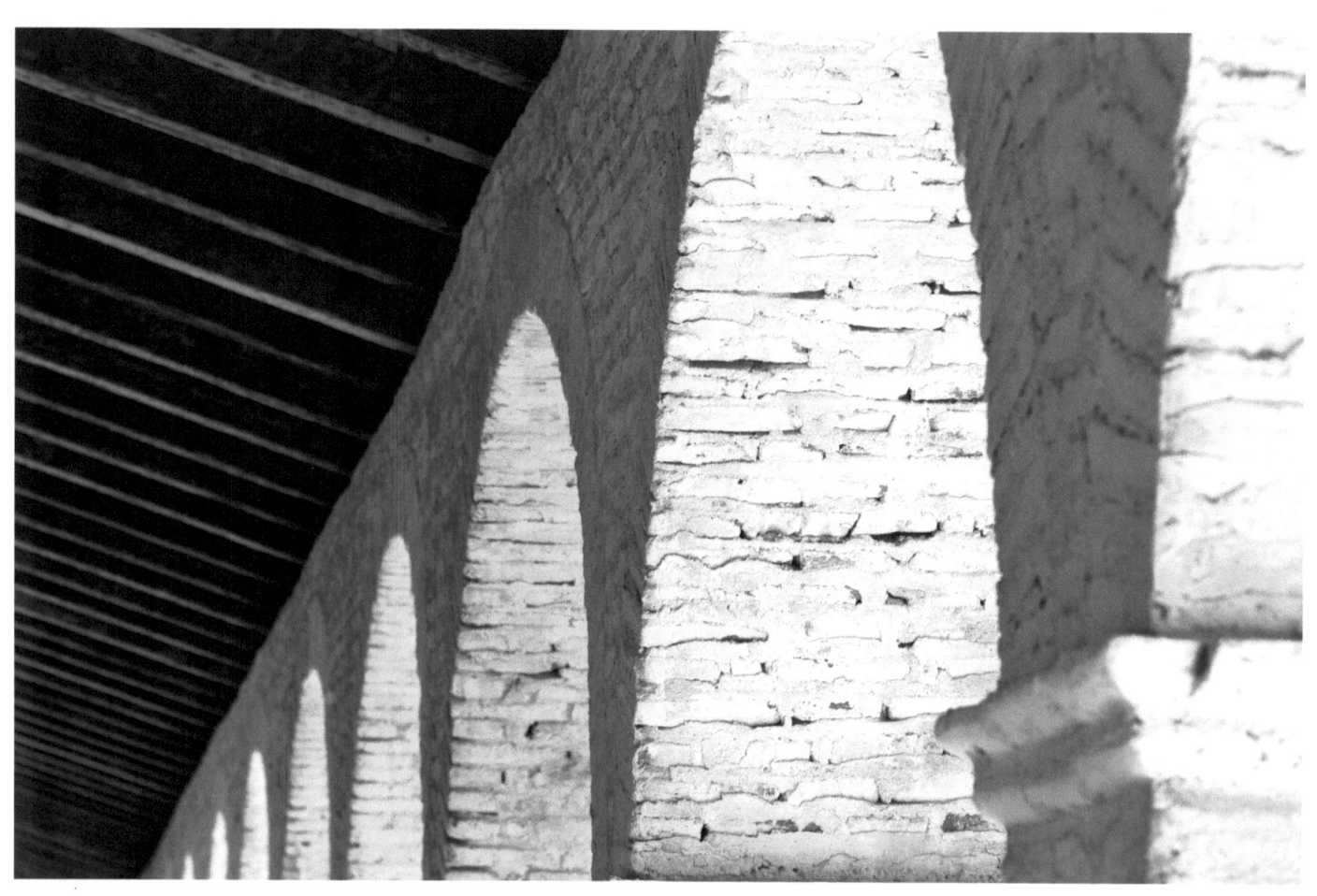

7656

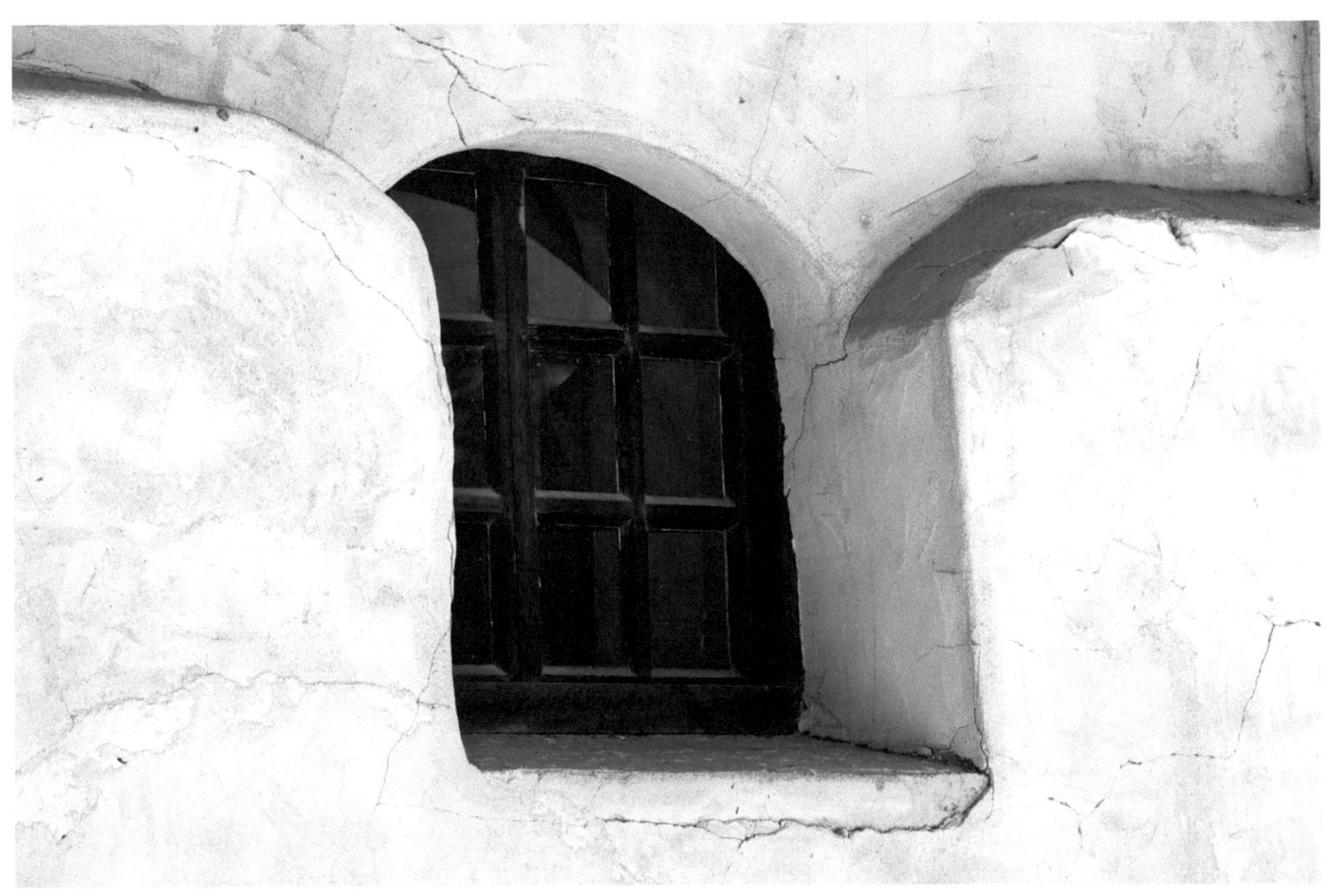

7693

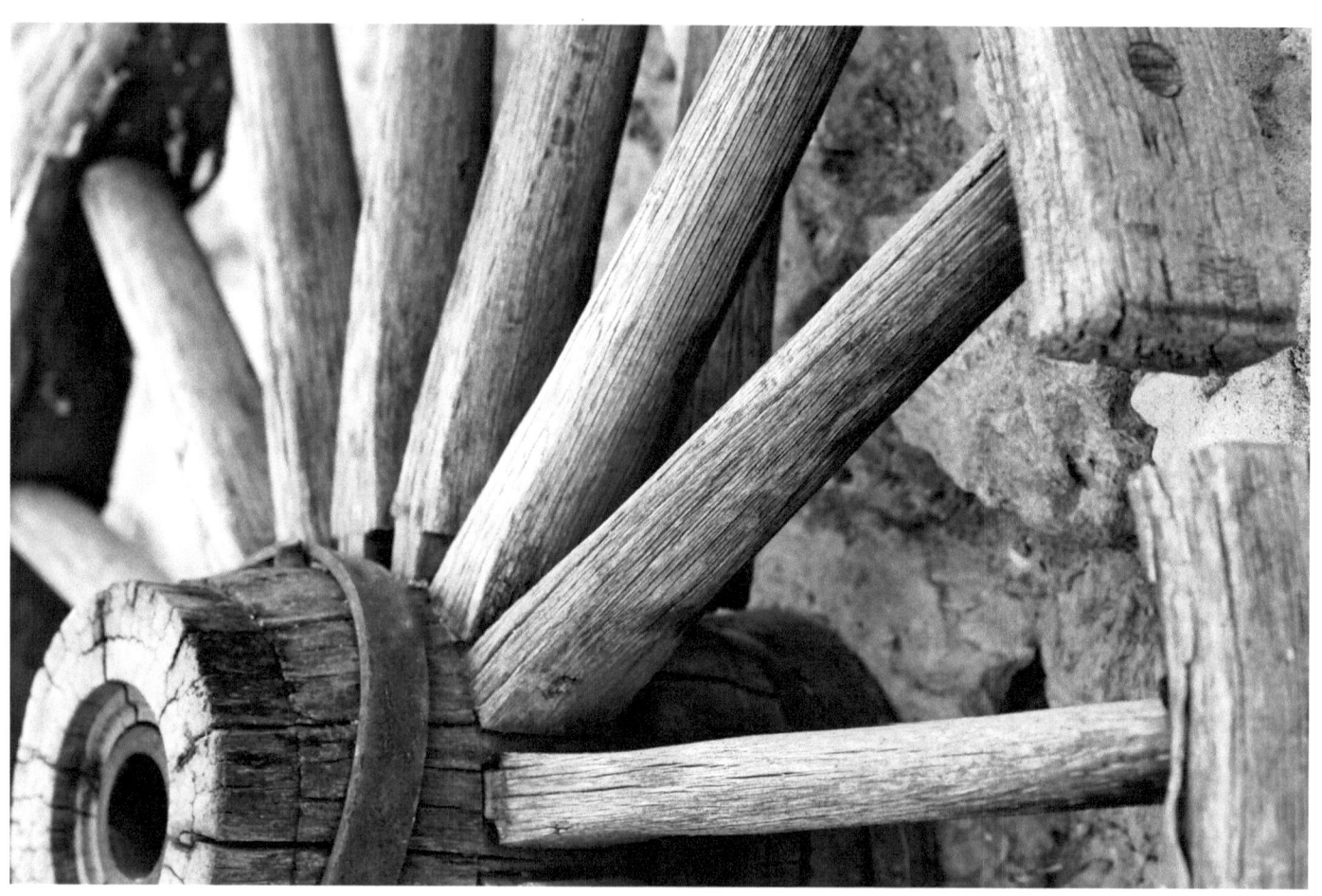

7783

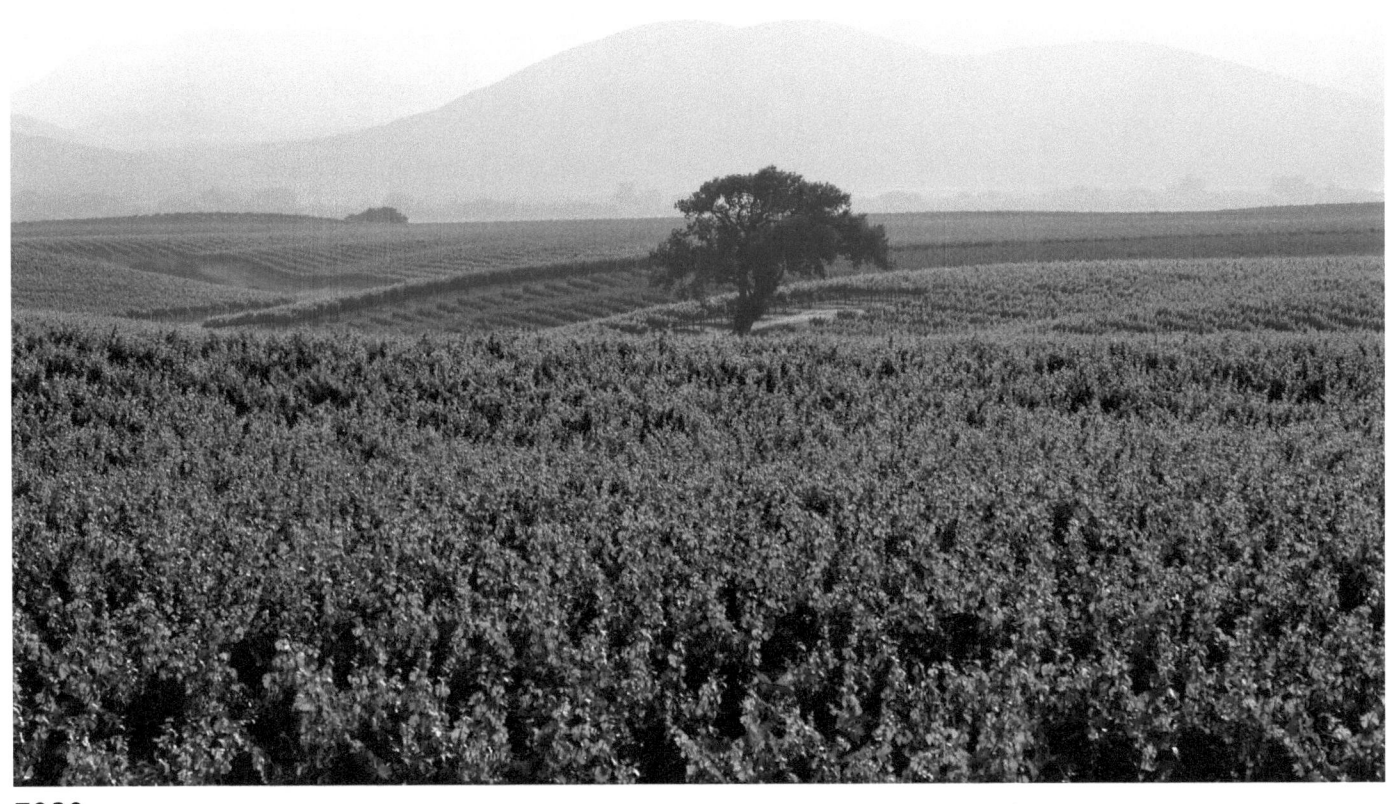

7939

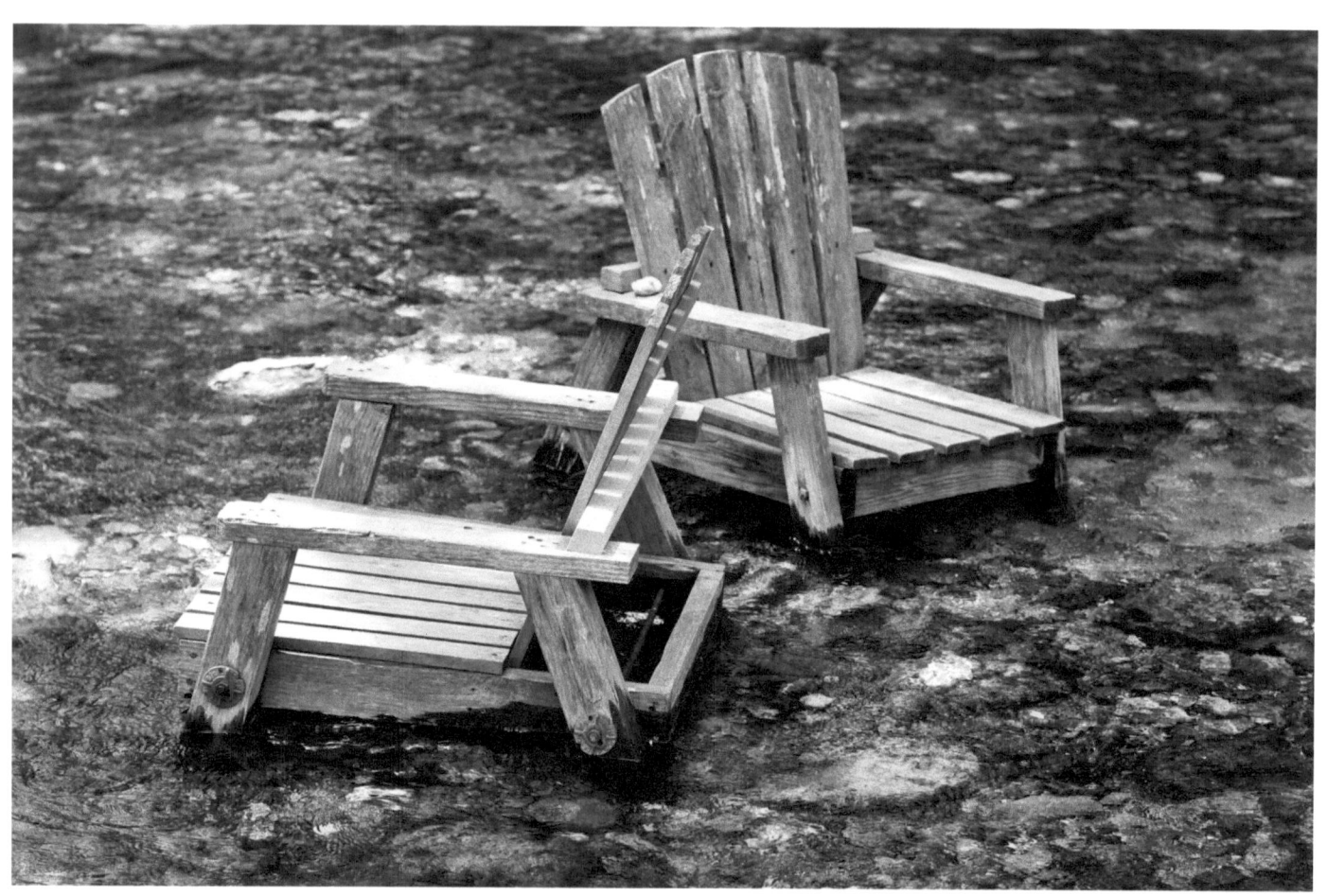

8173

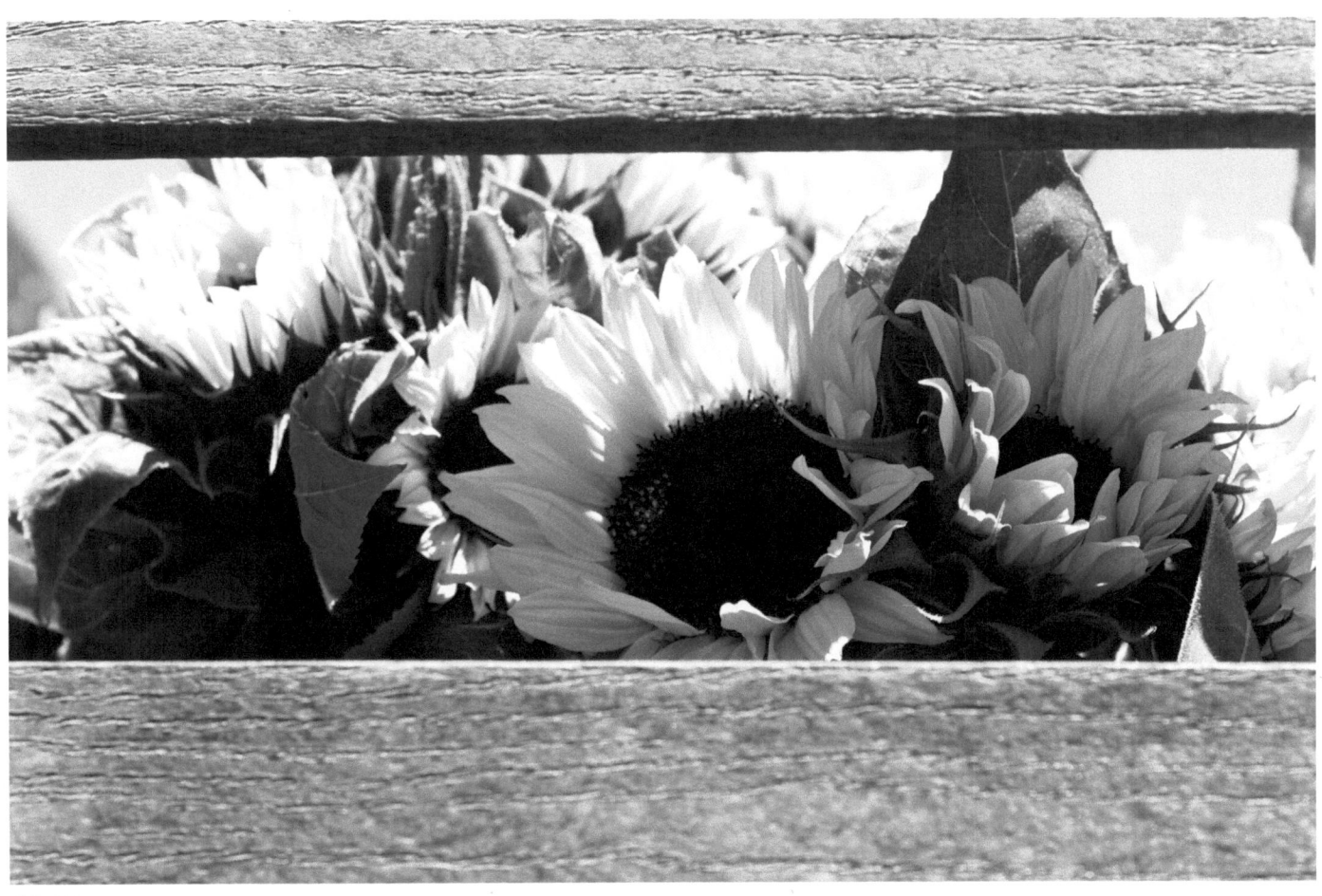

8345

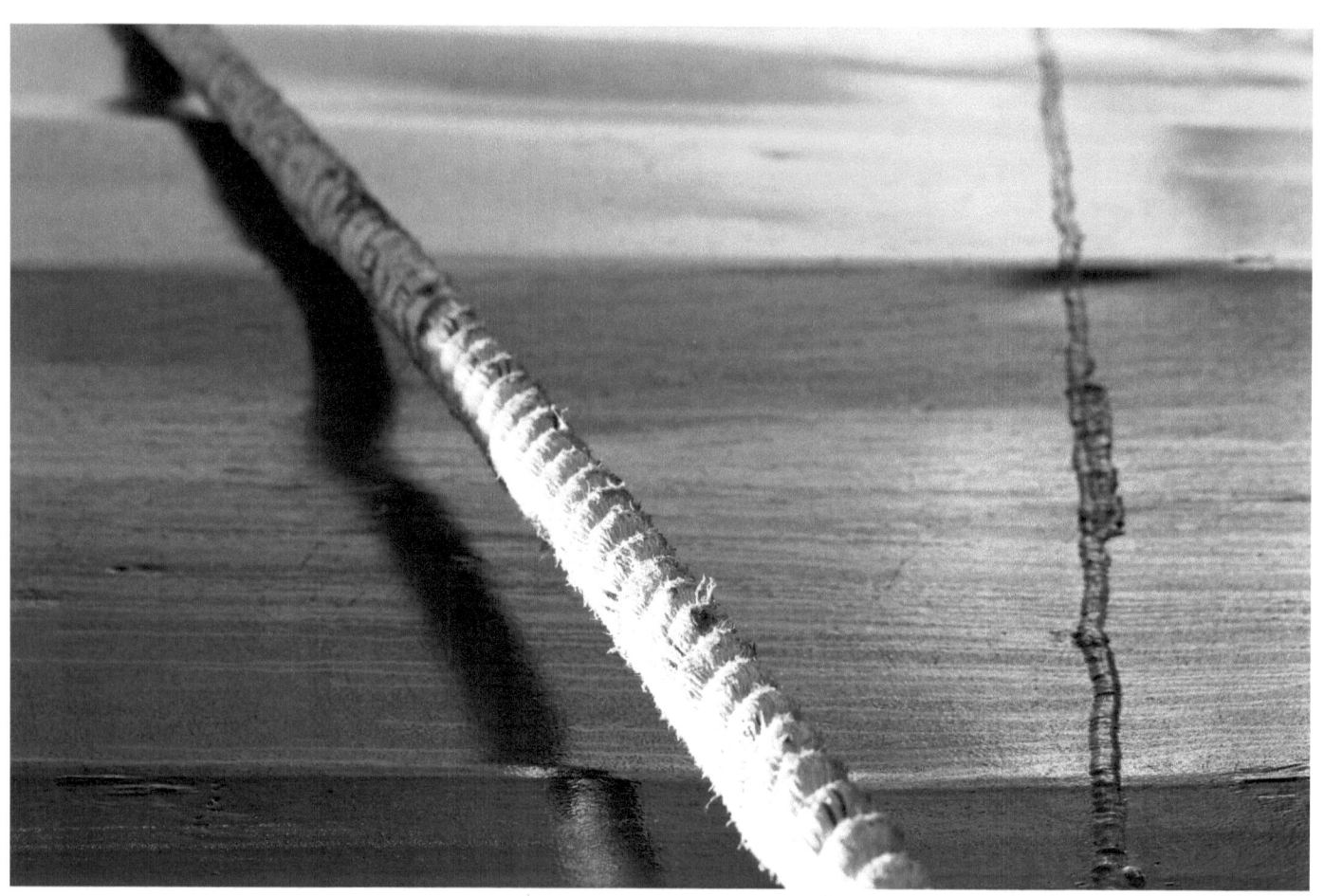

8470

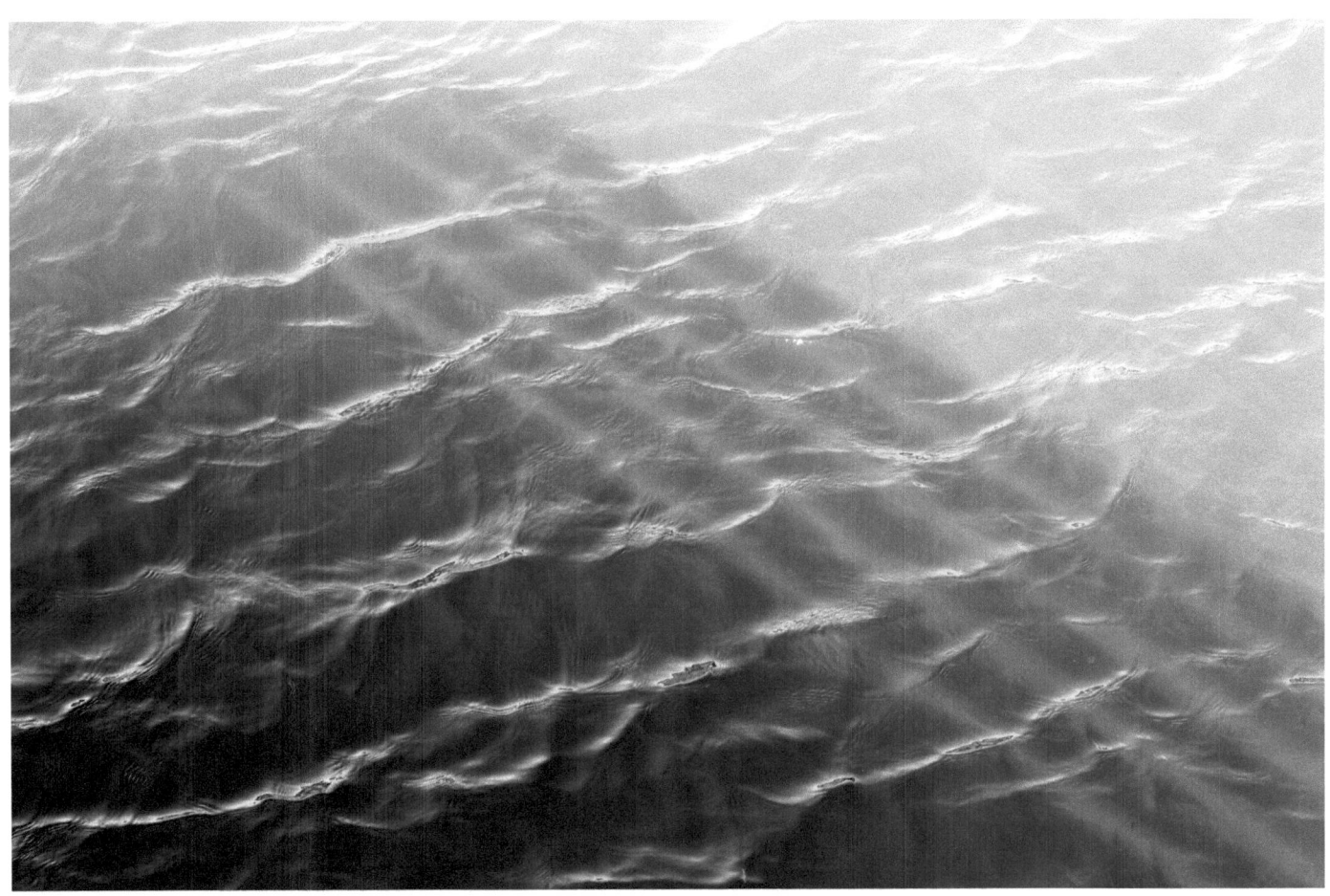

8471

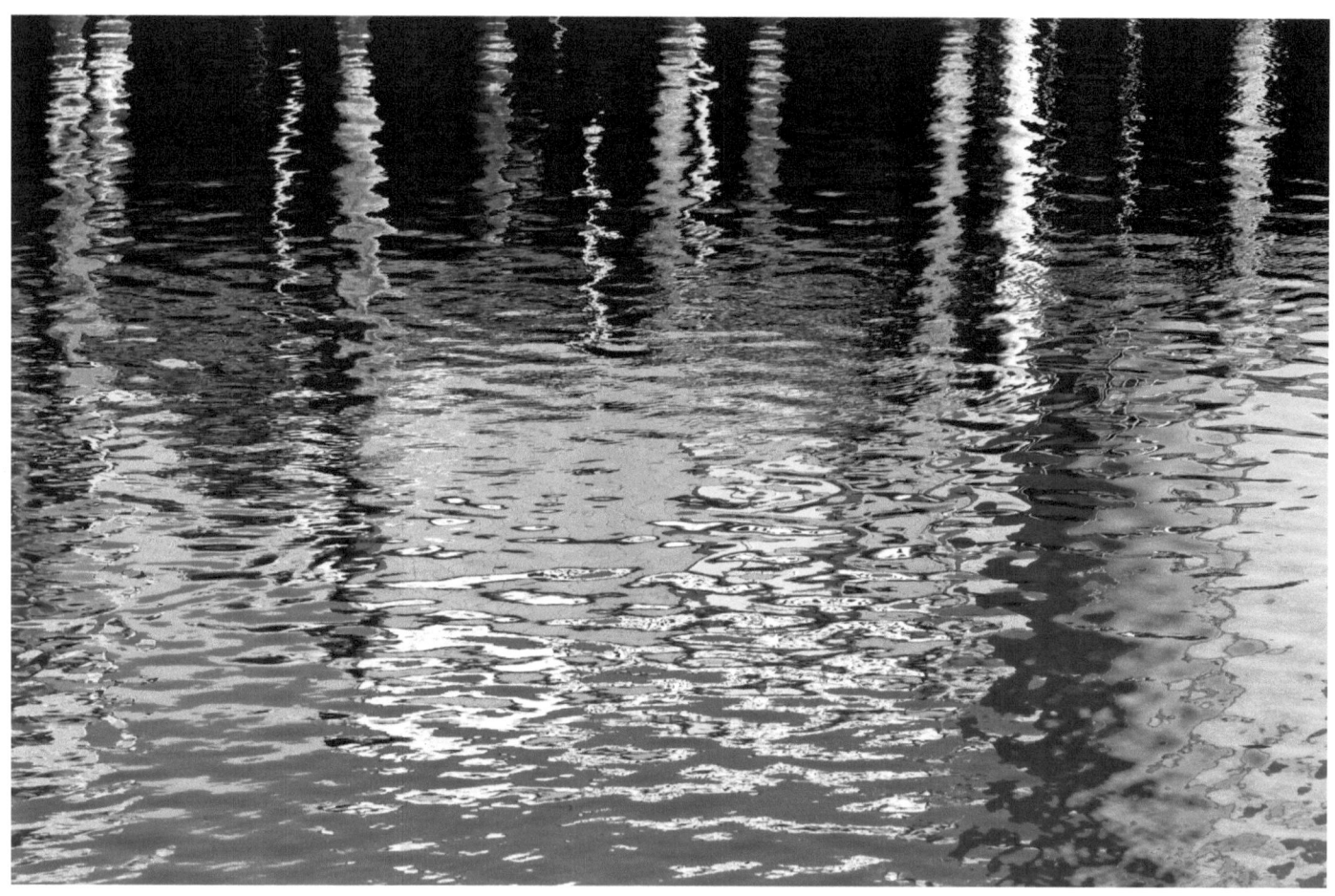

8766

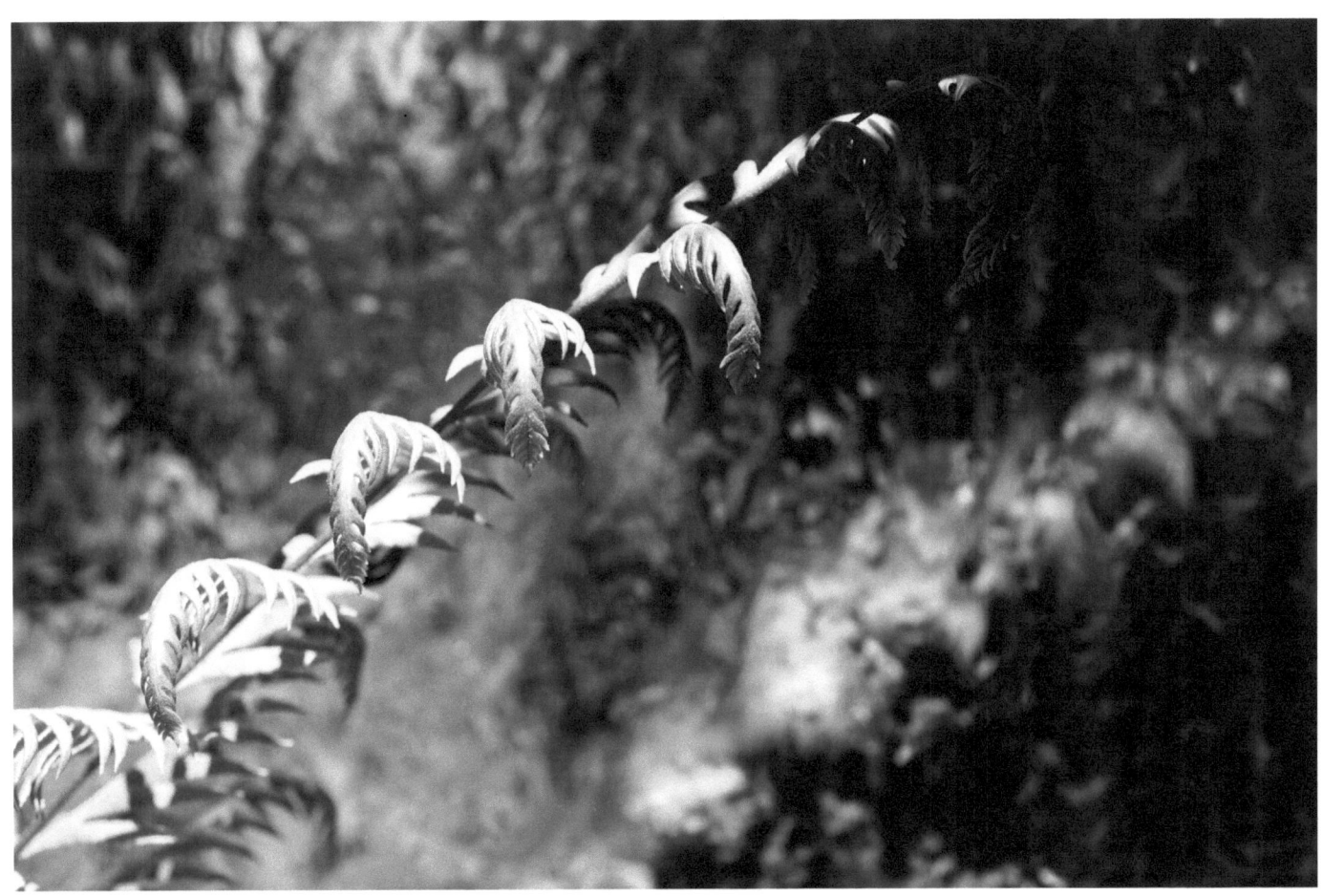

8889

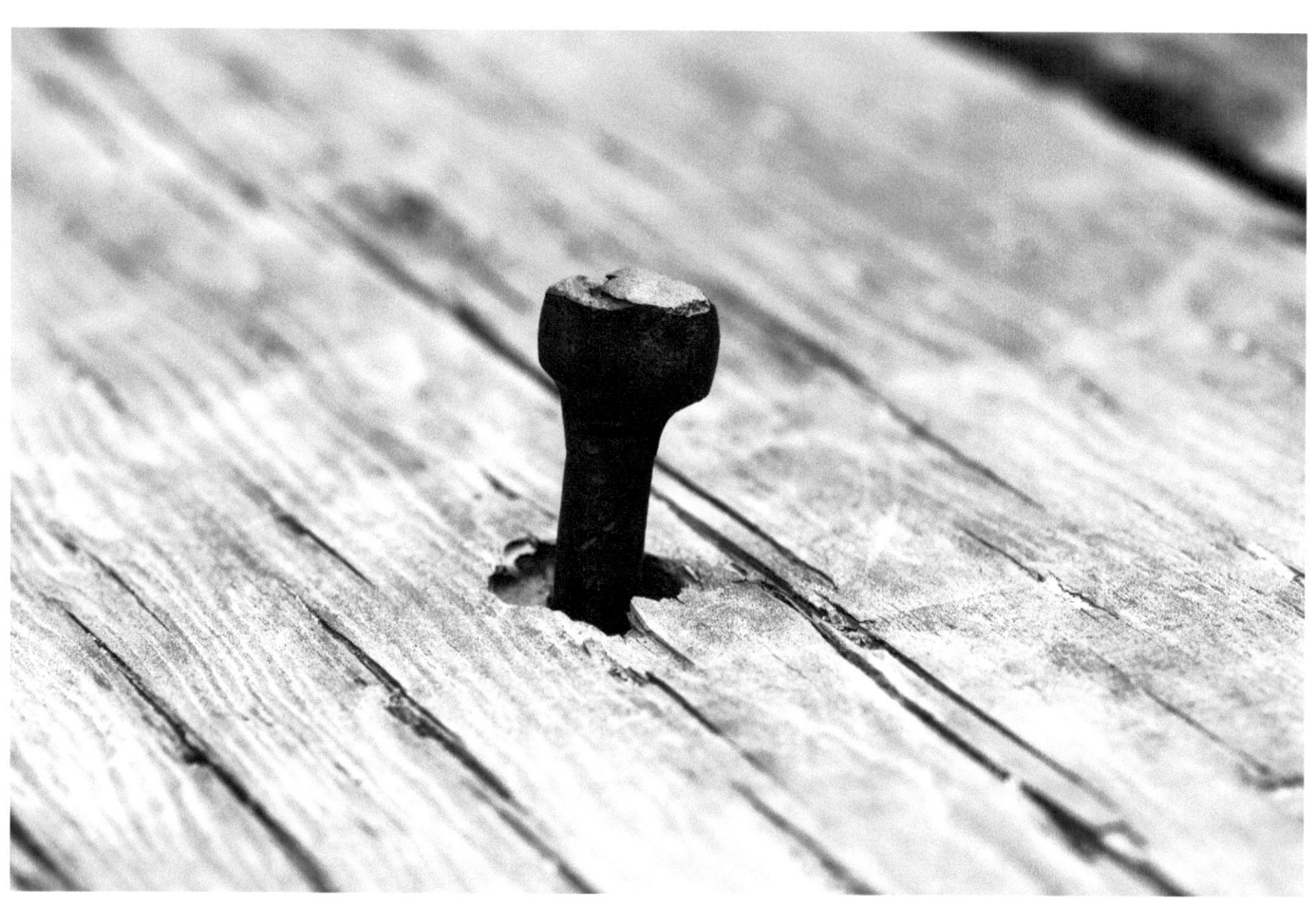

9024

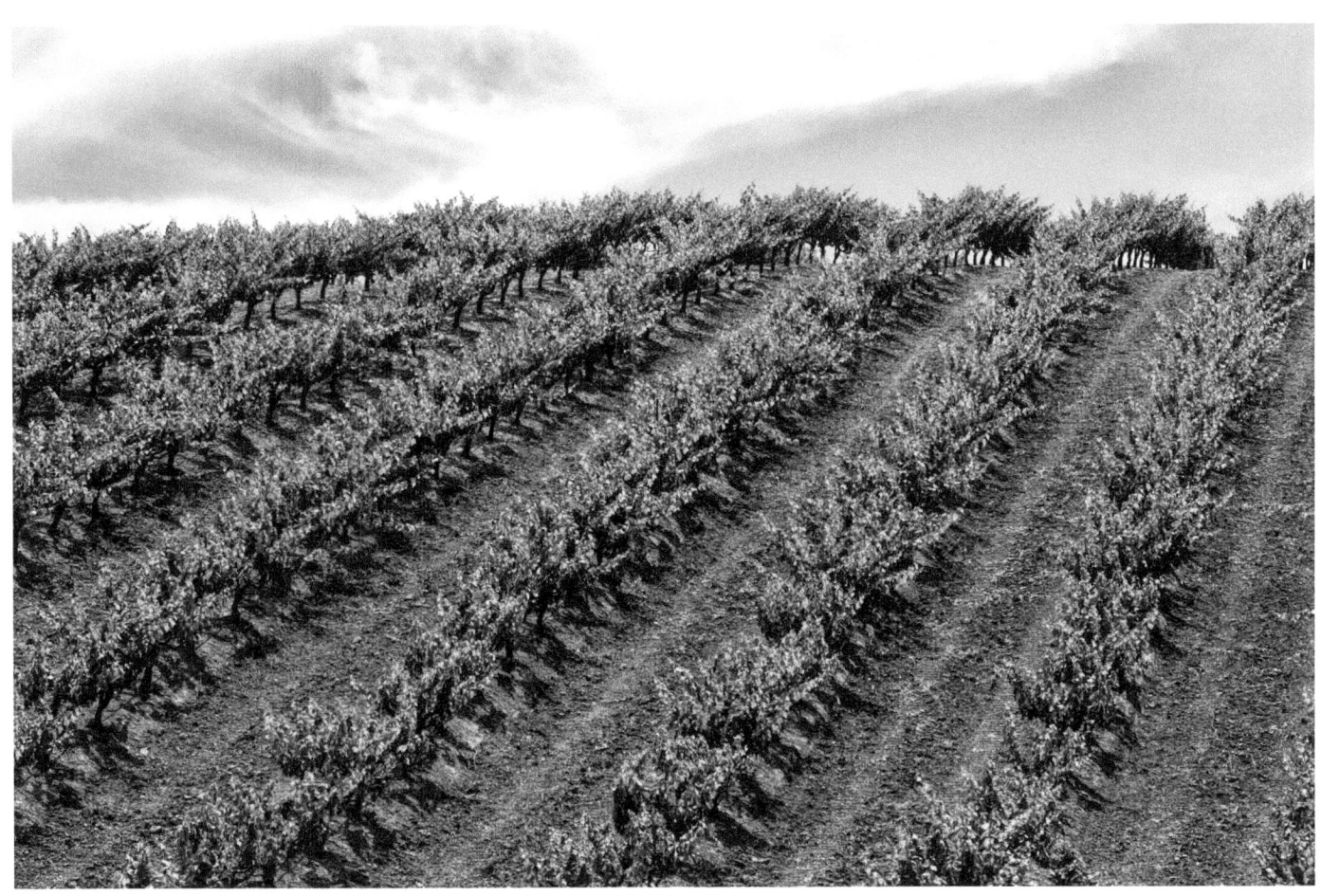

9297

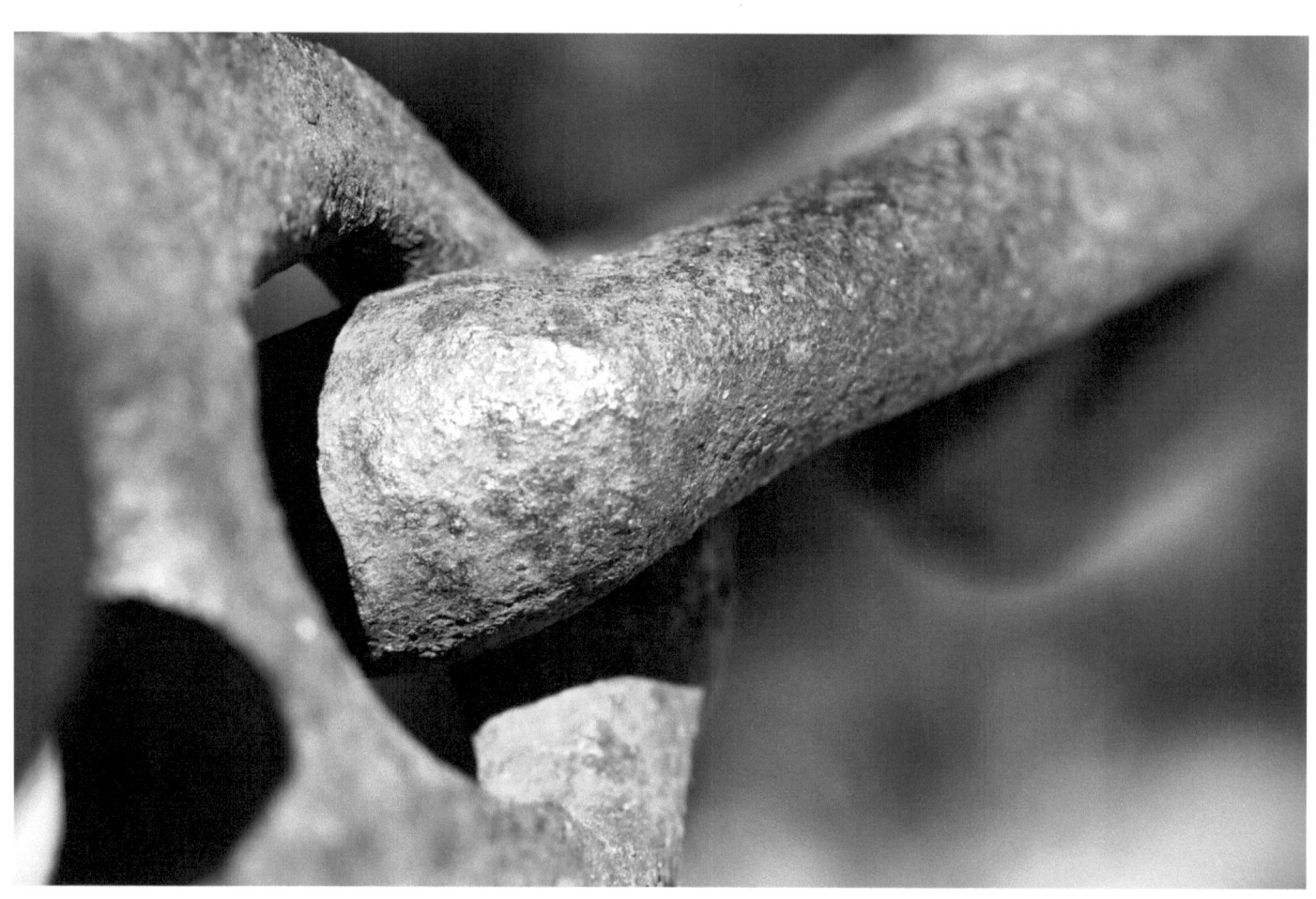

9353

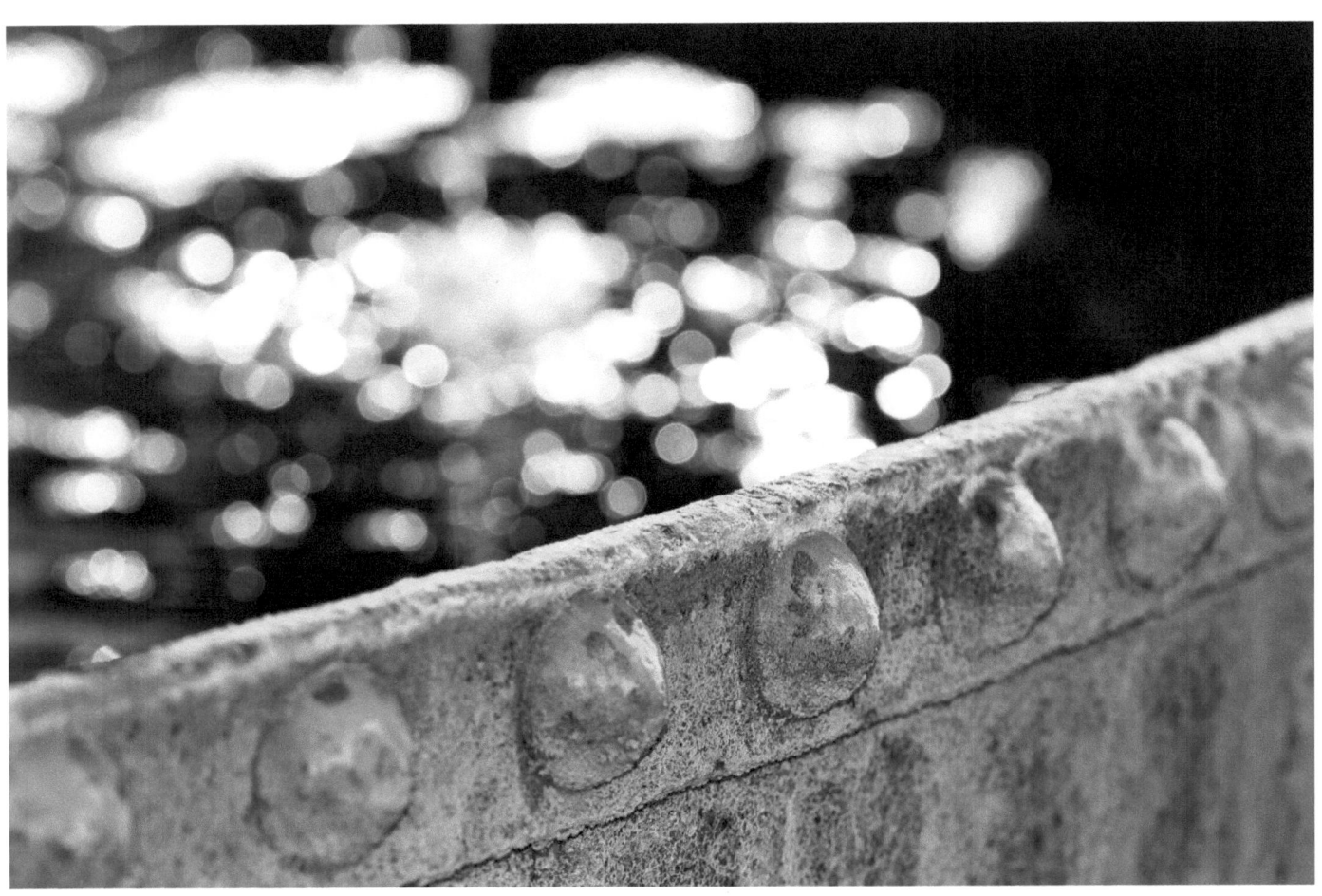

9430

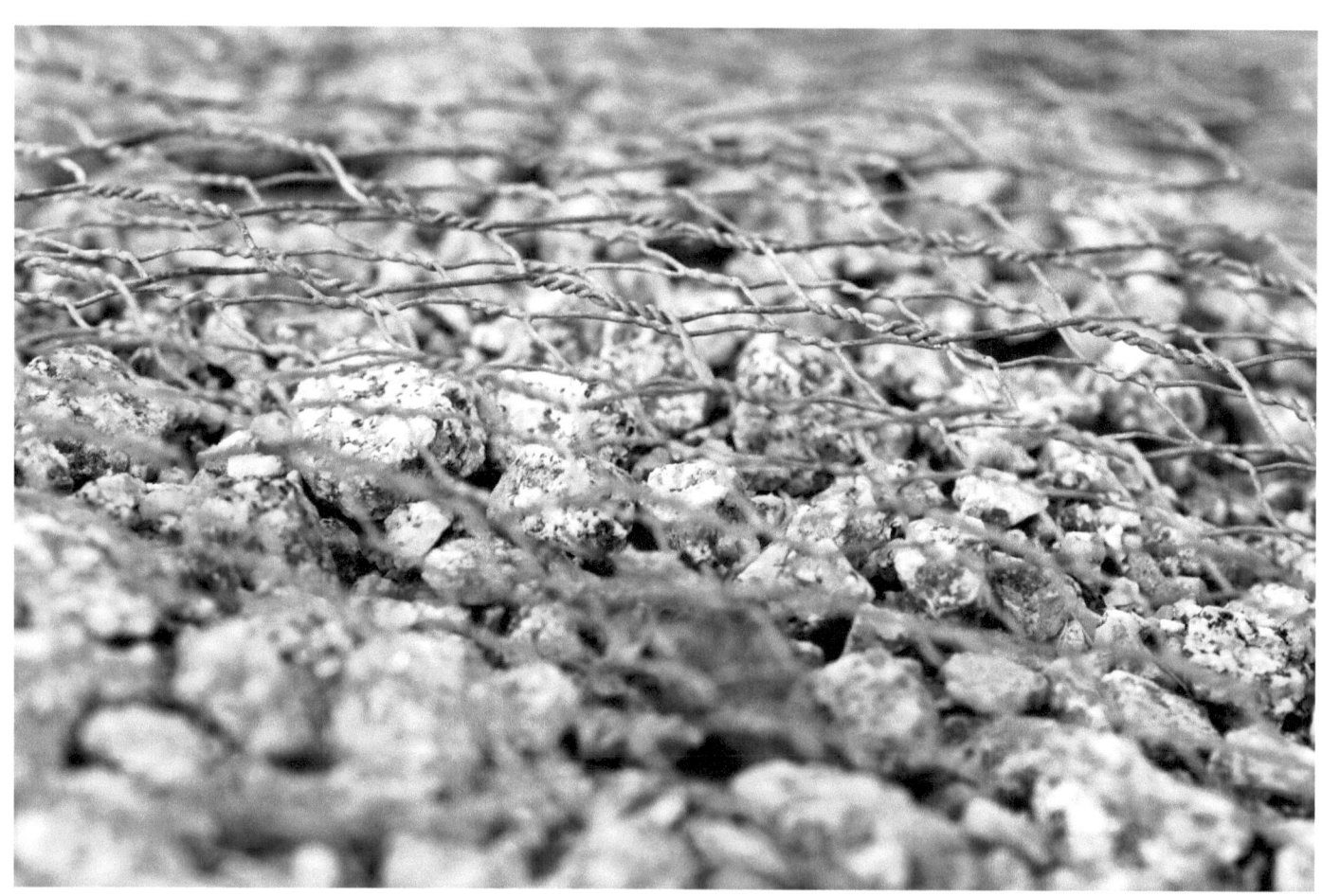

9970

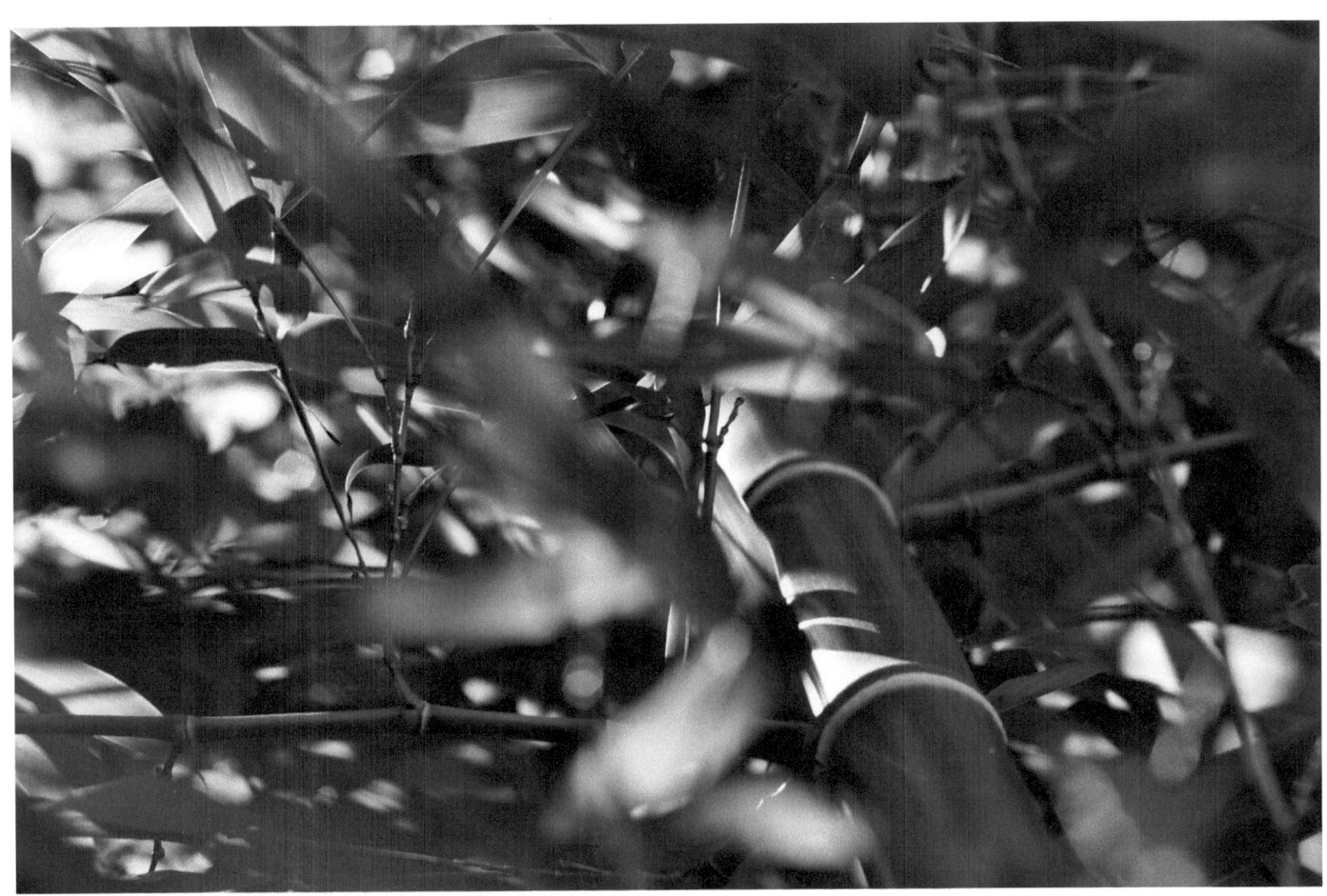

9975

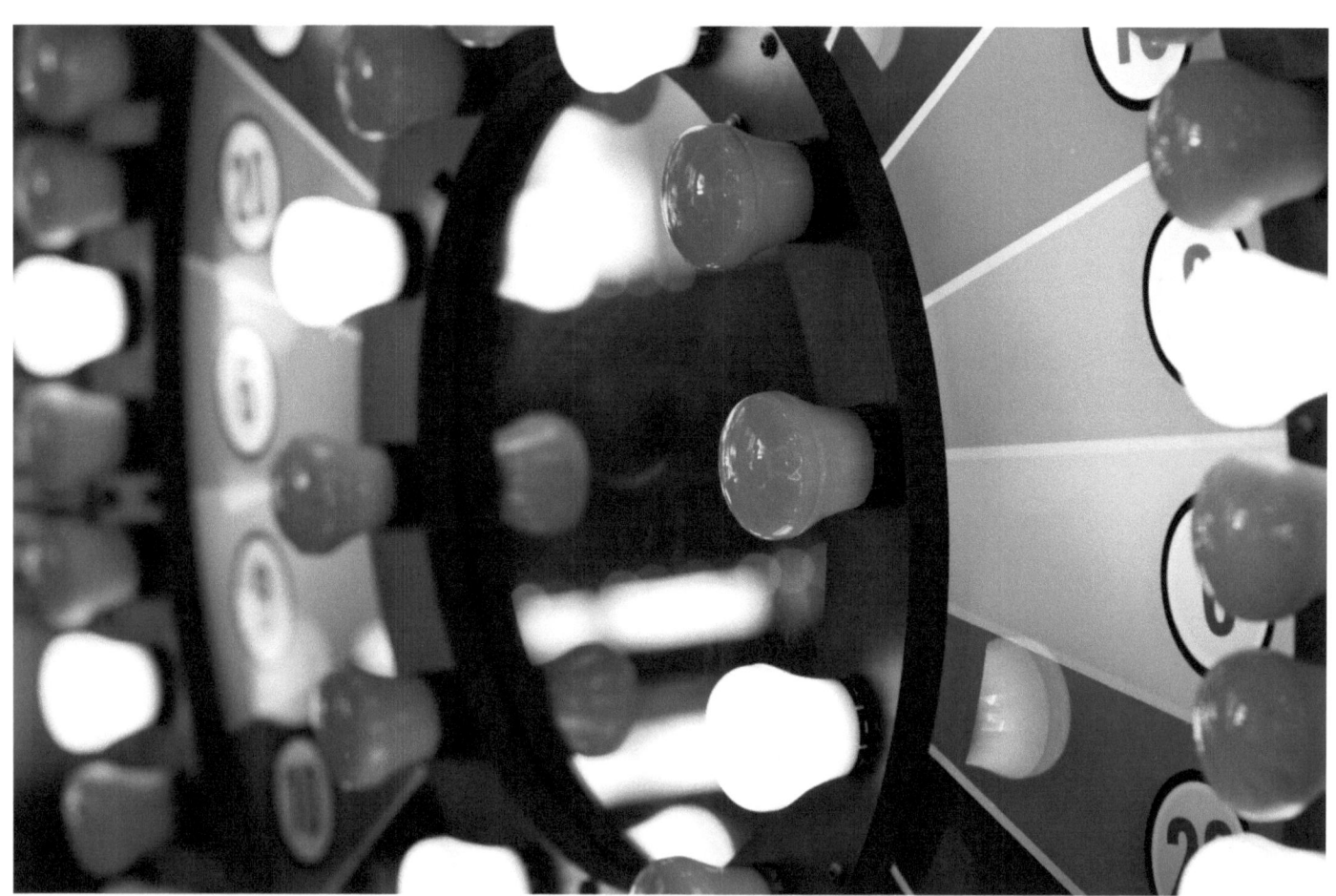

9980

9992

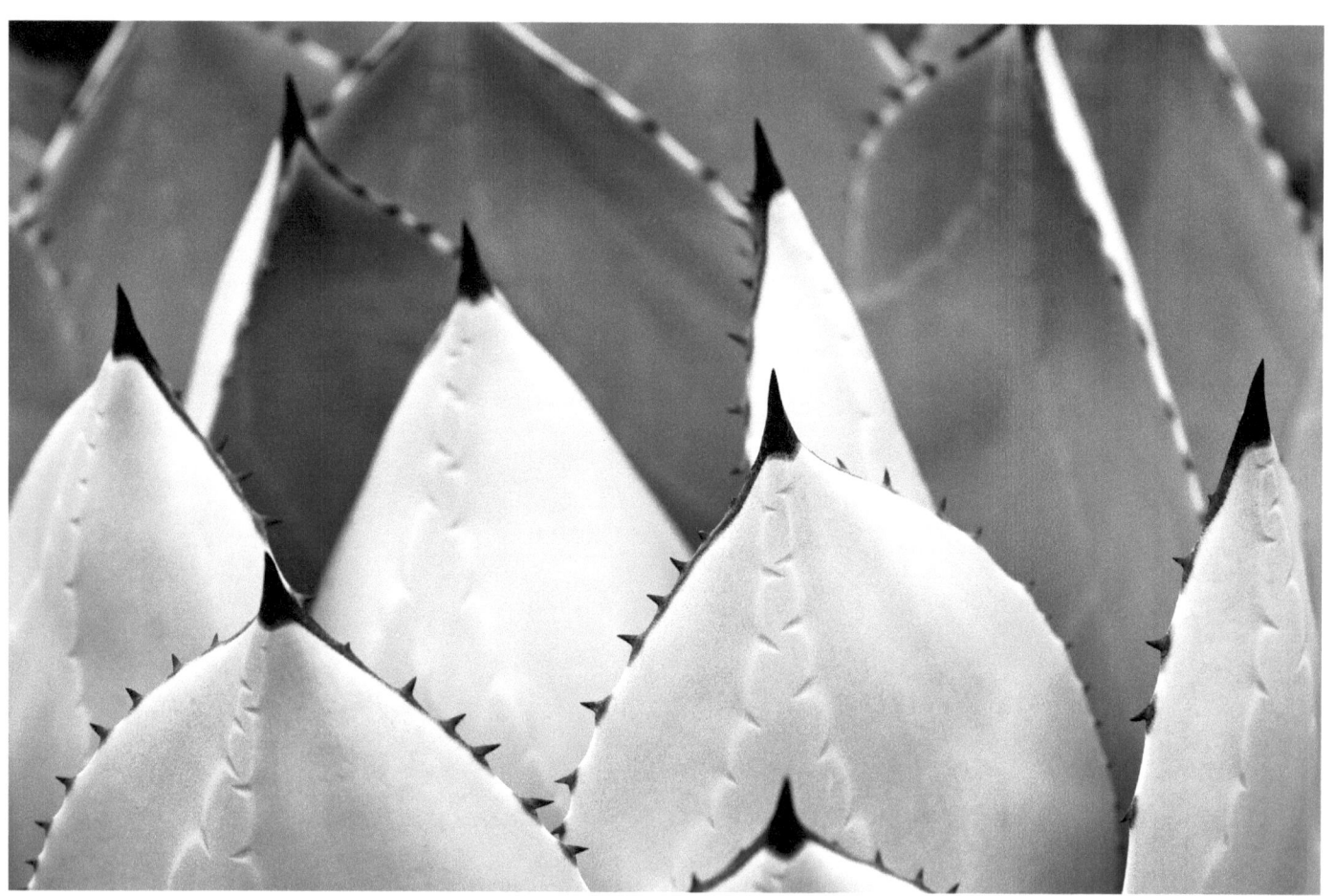

9993

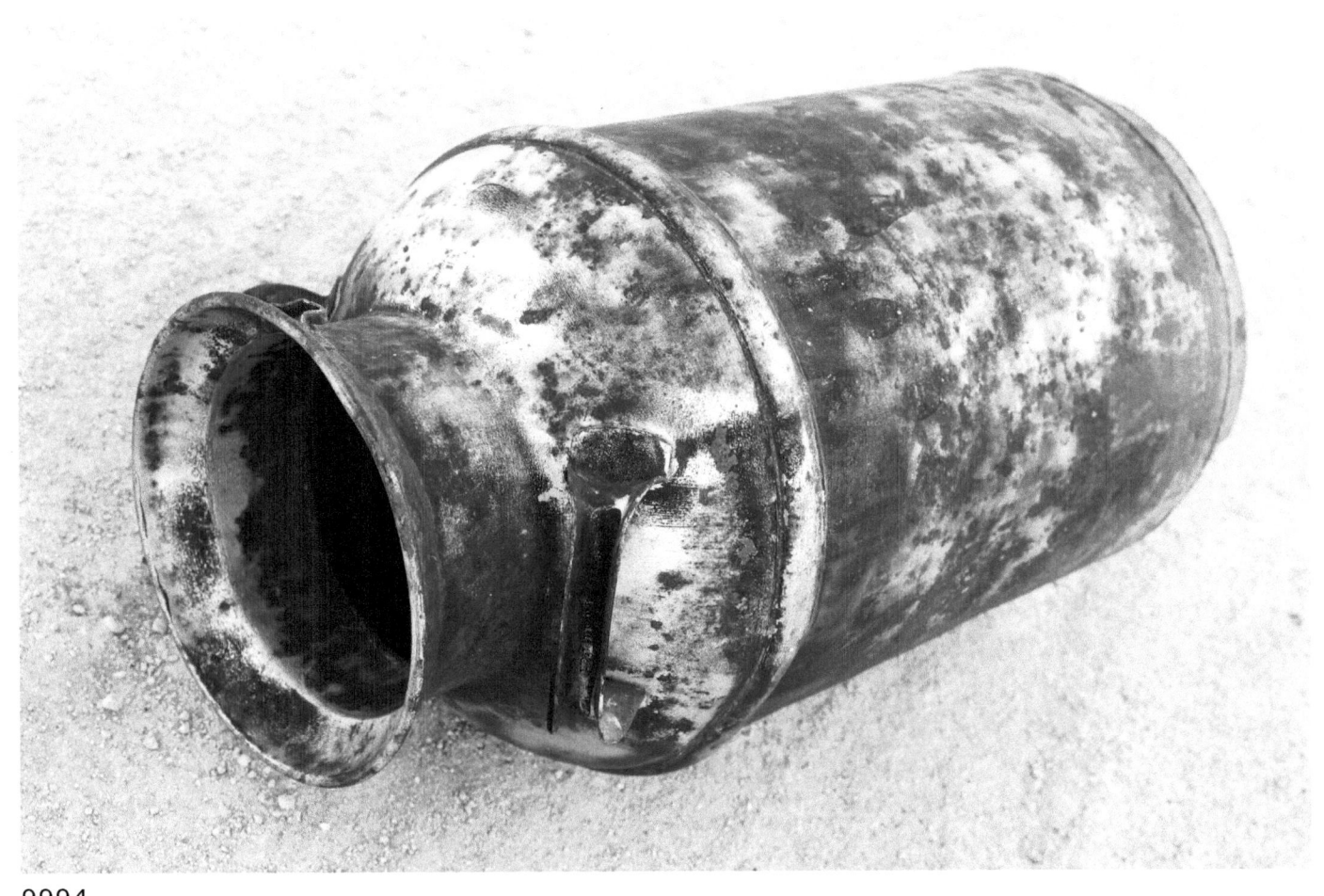

9994

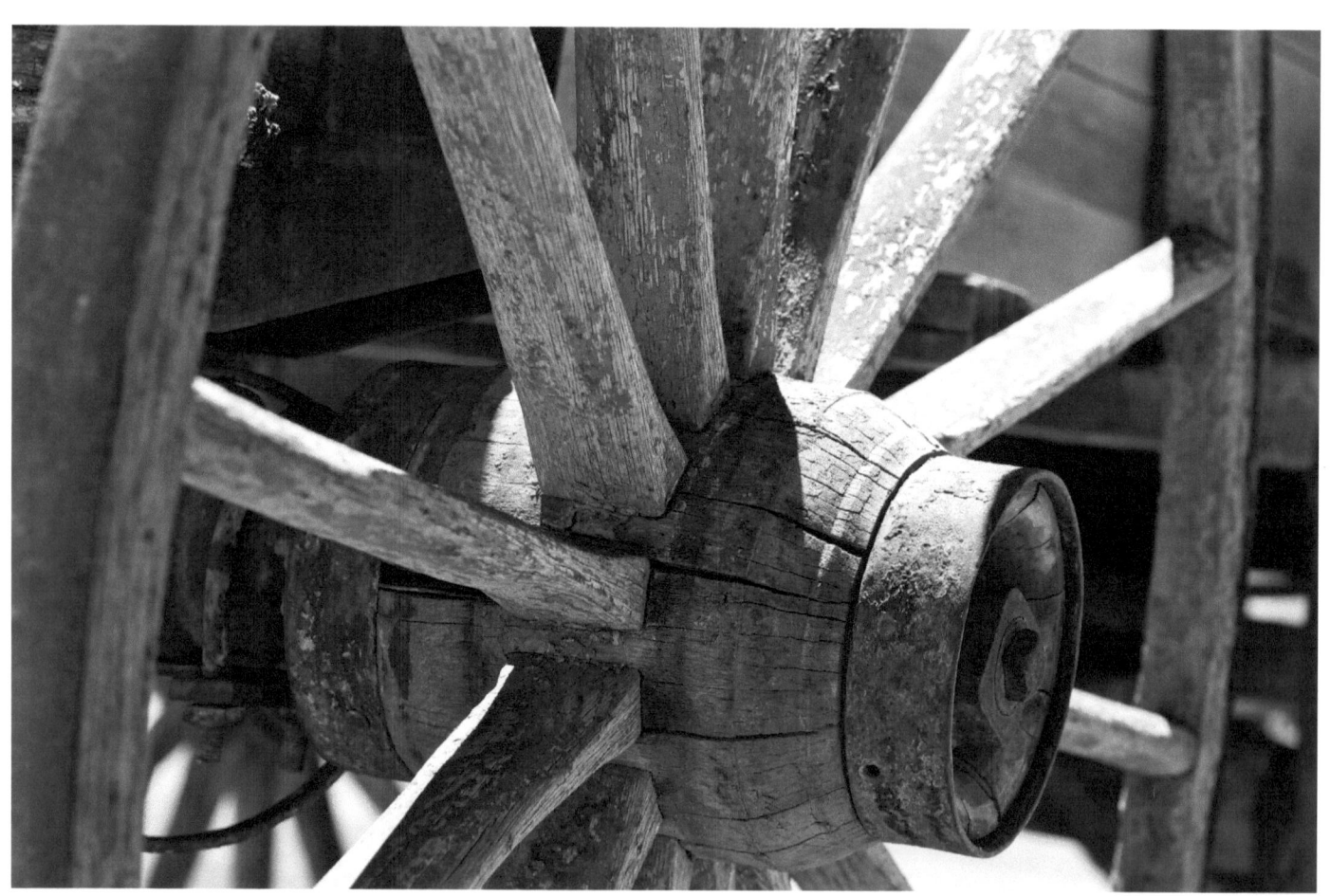

9995

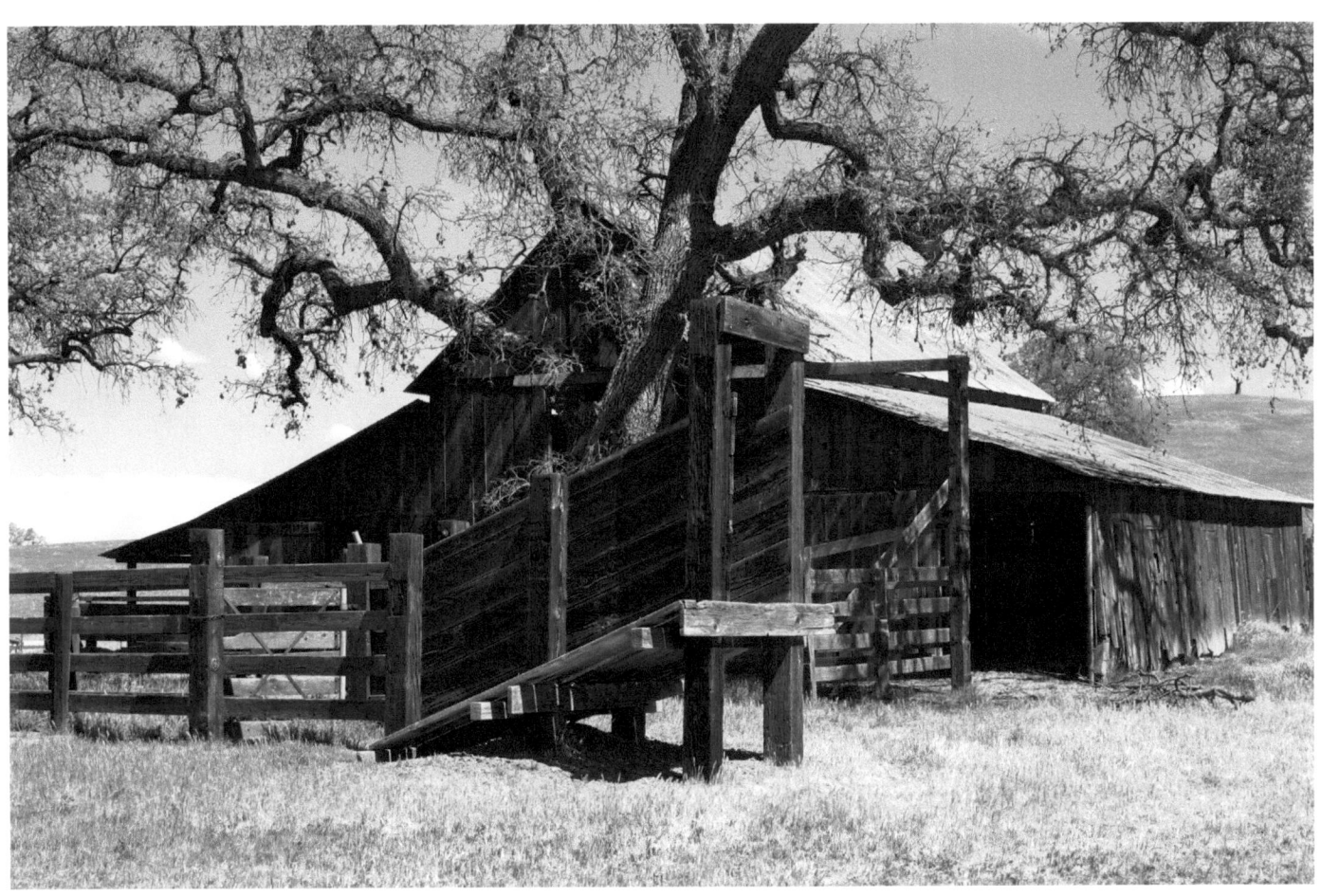

9996

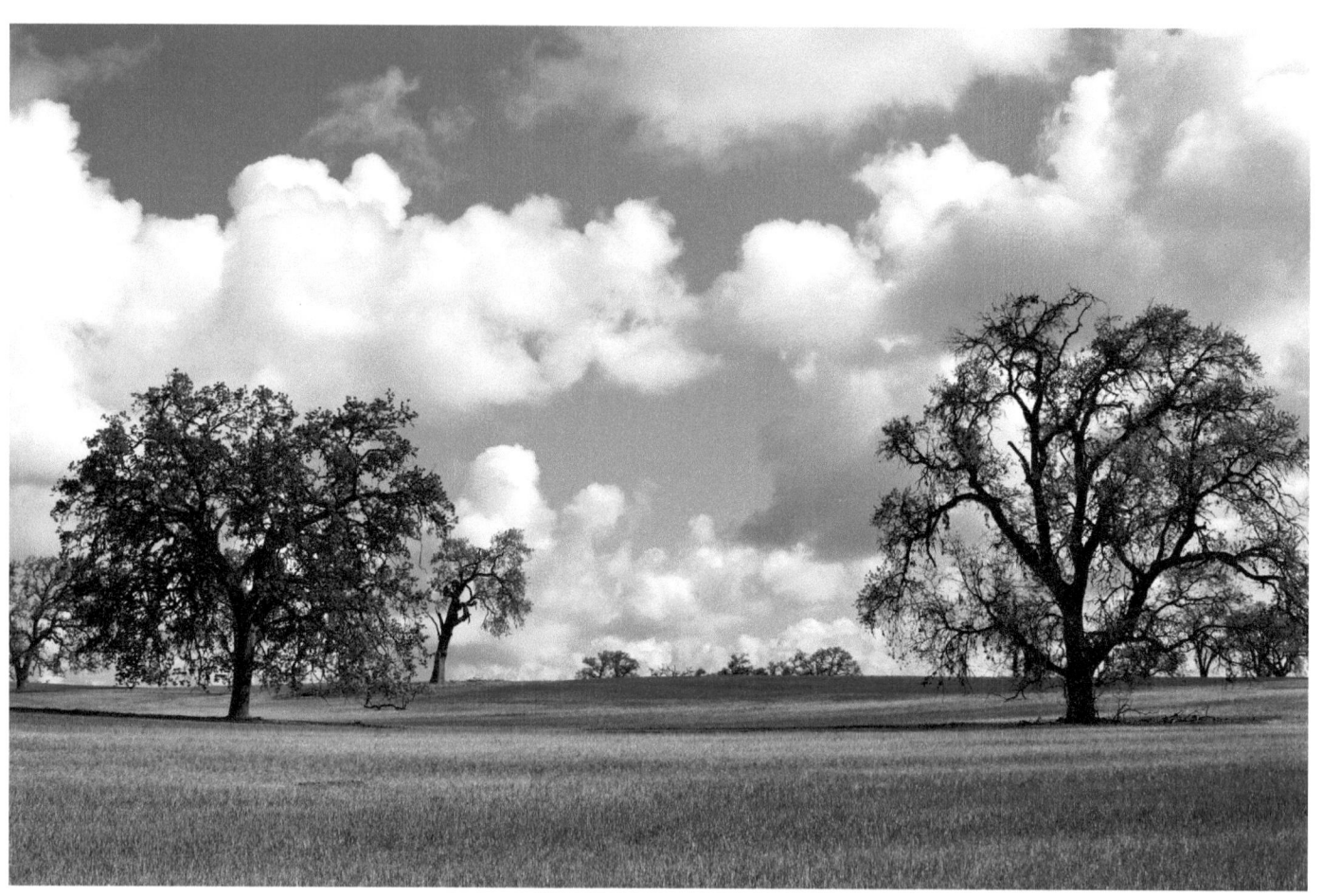

9997

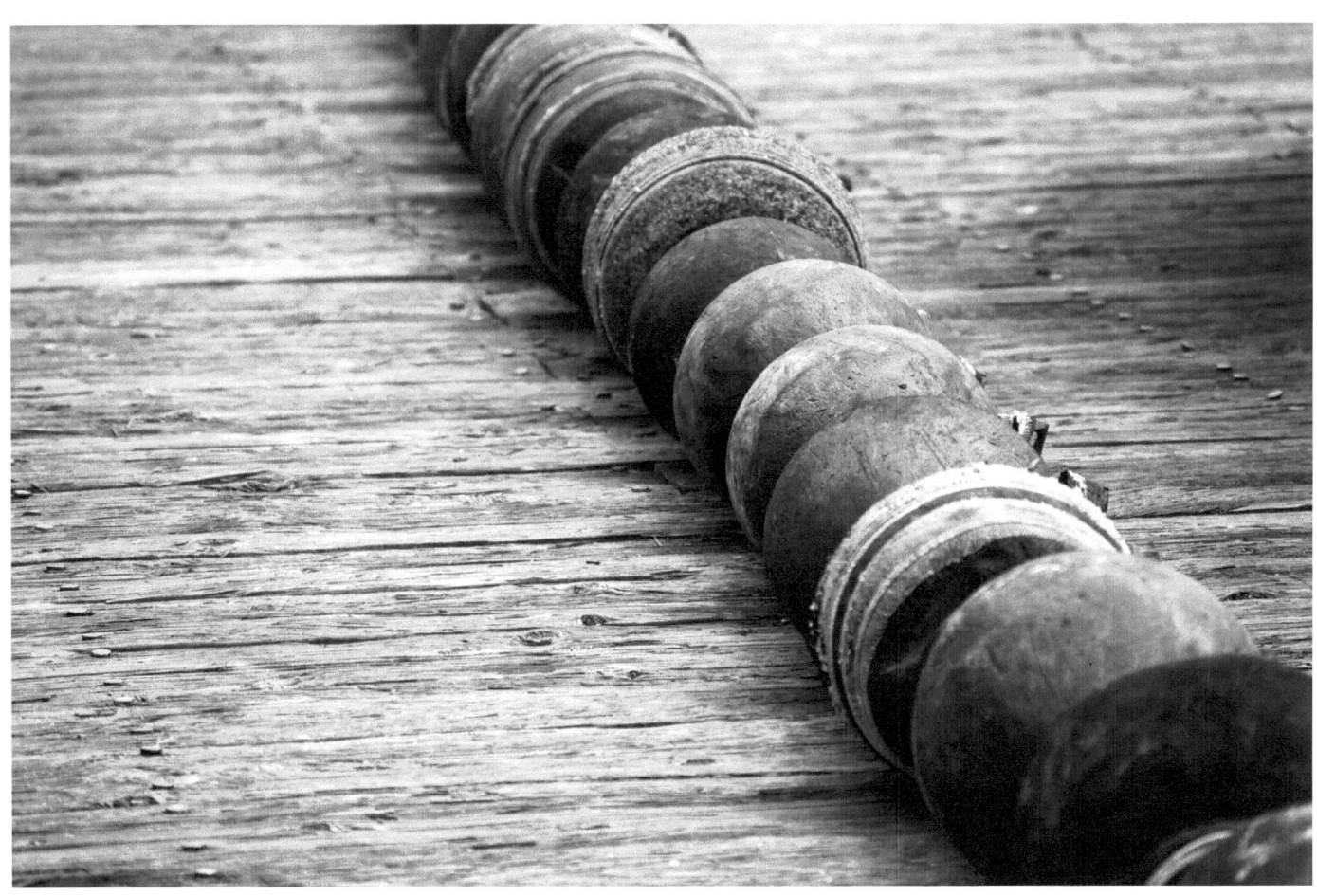

9998

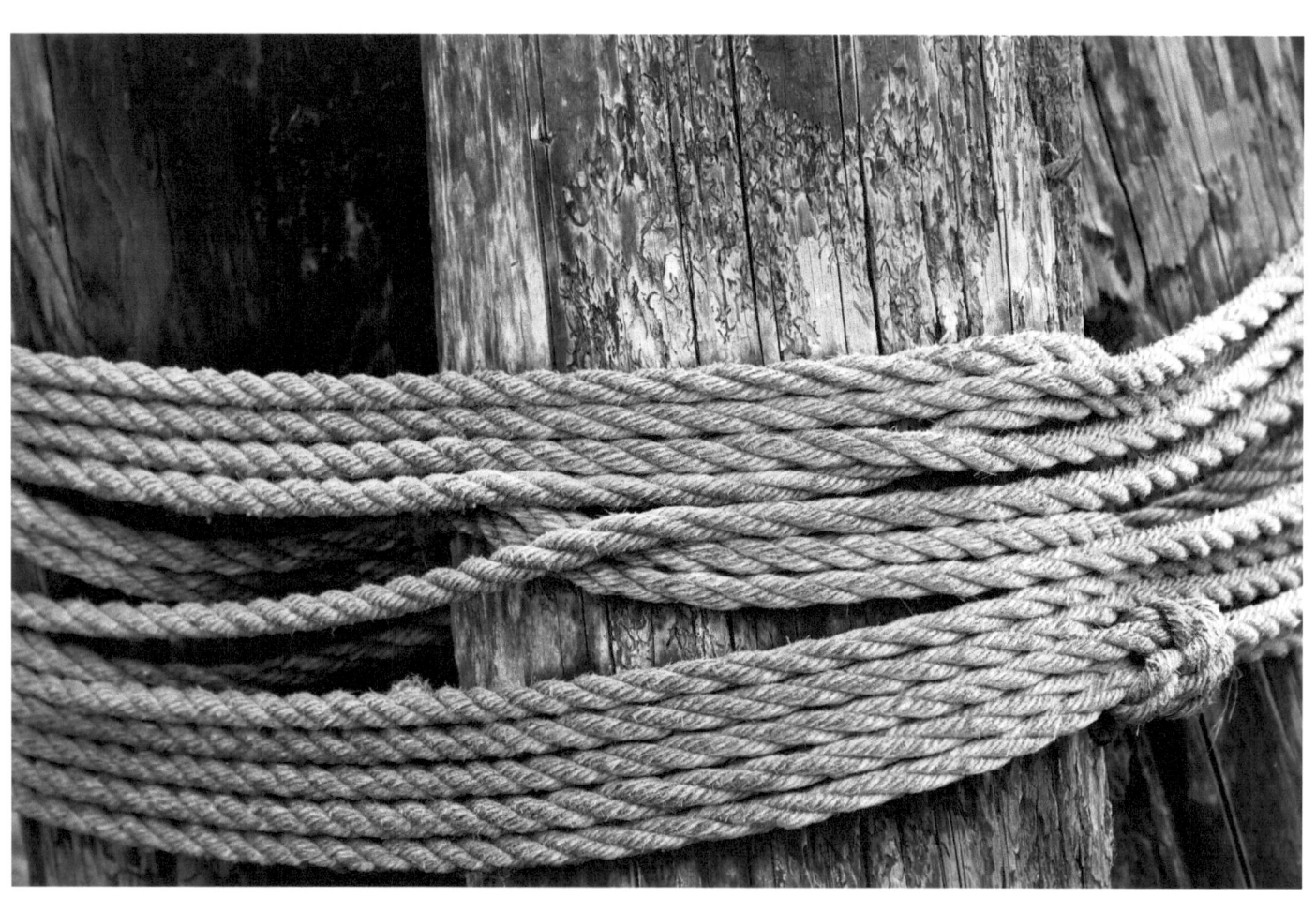

9999

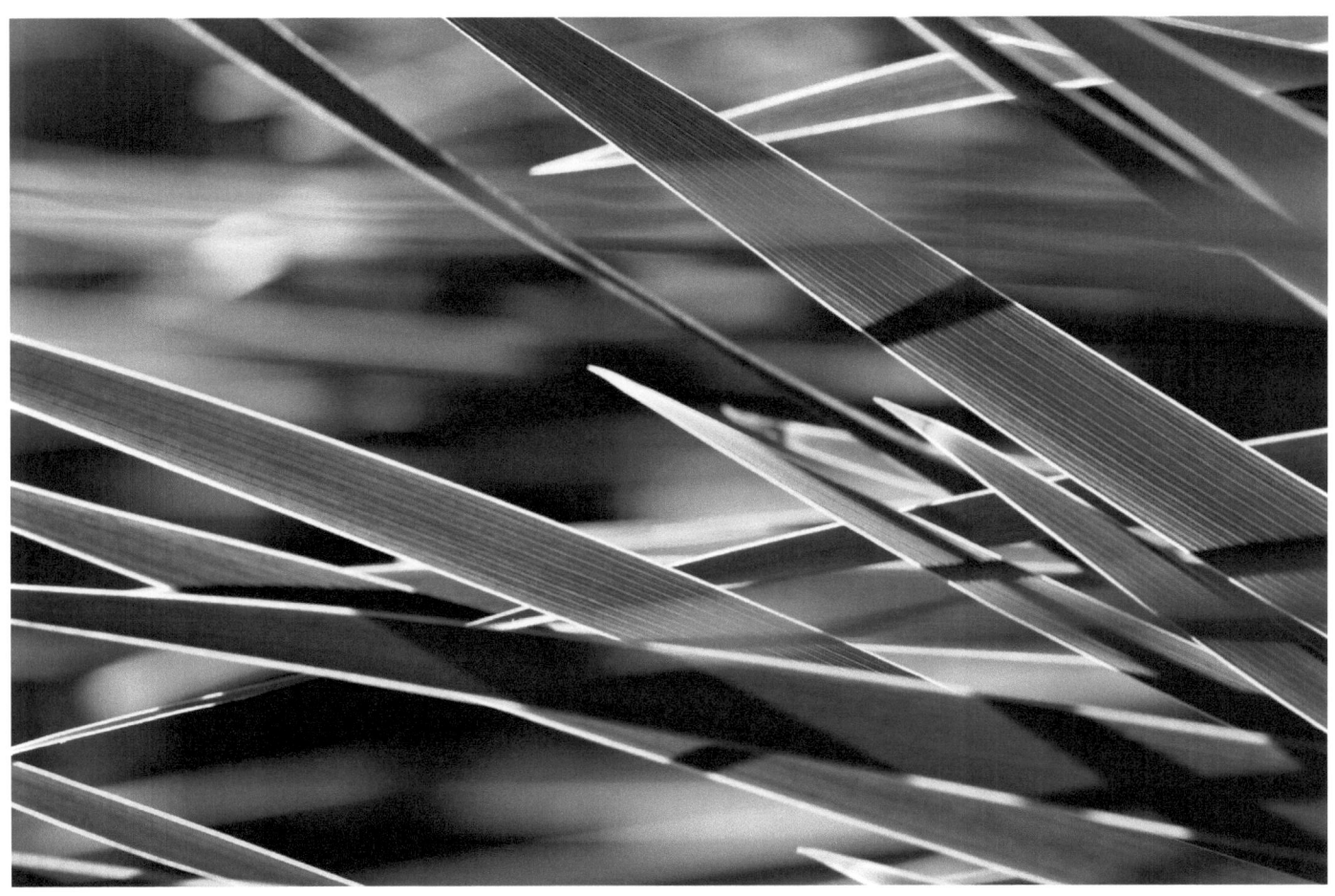

10000

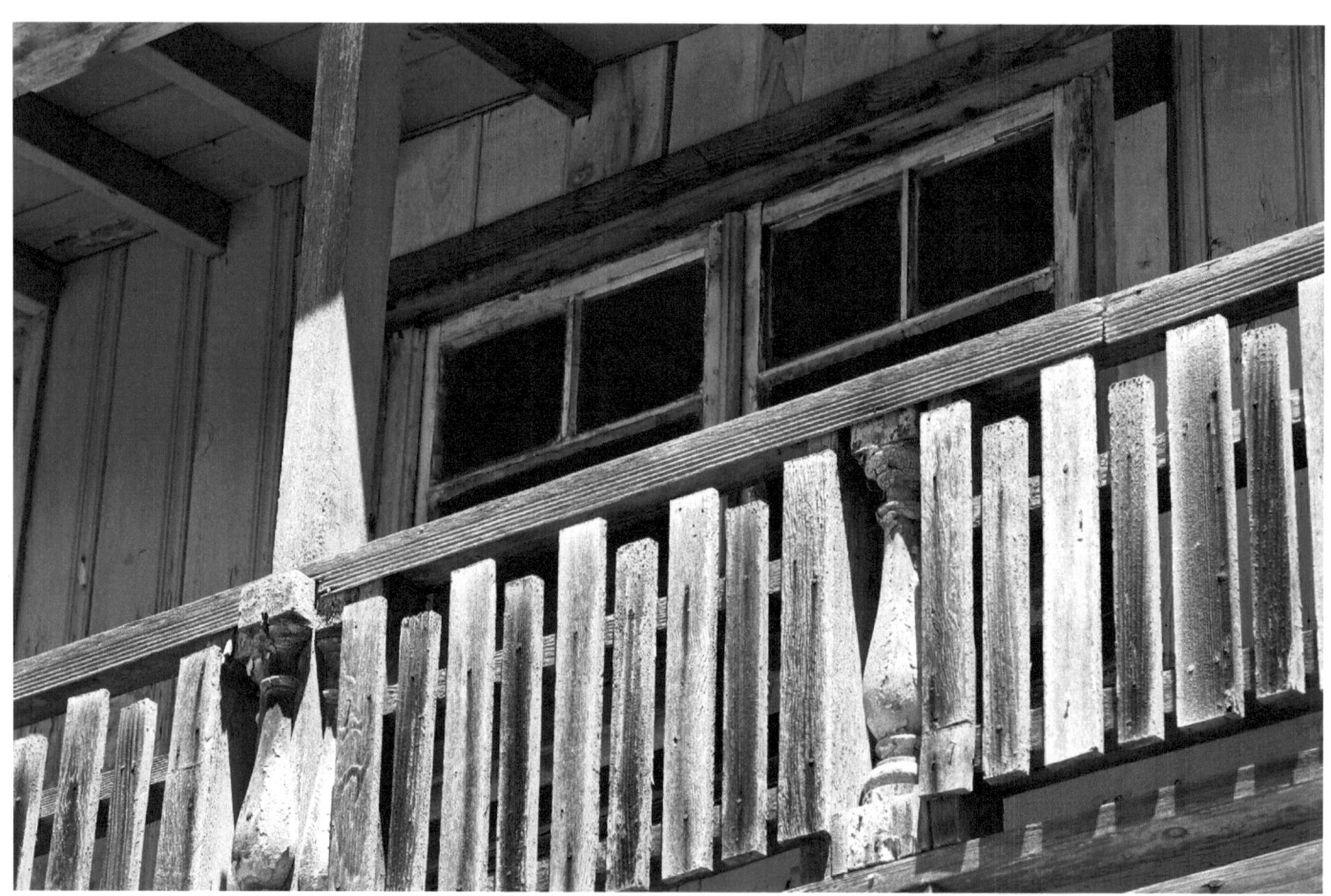

10001

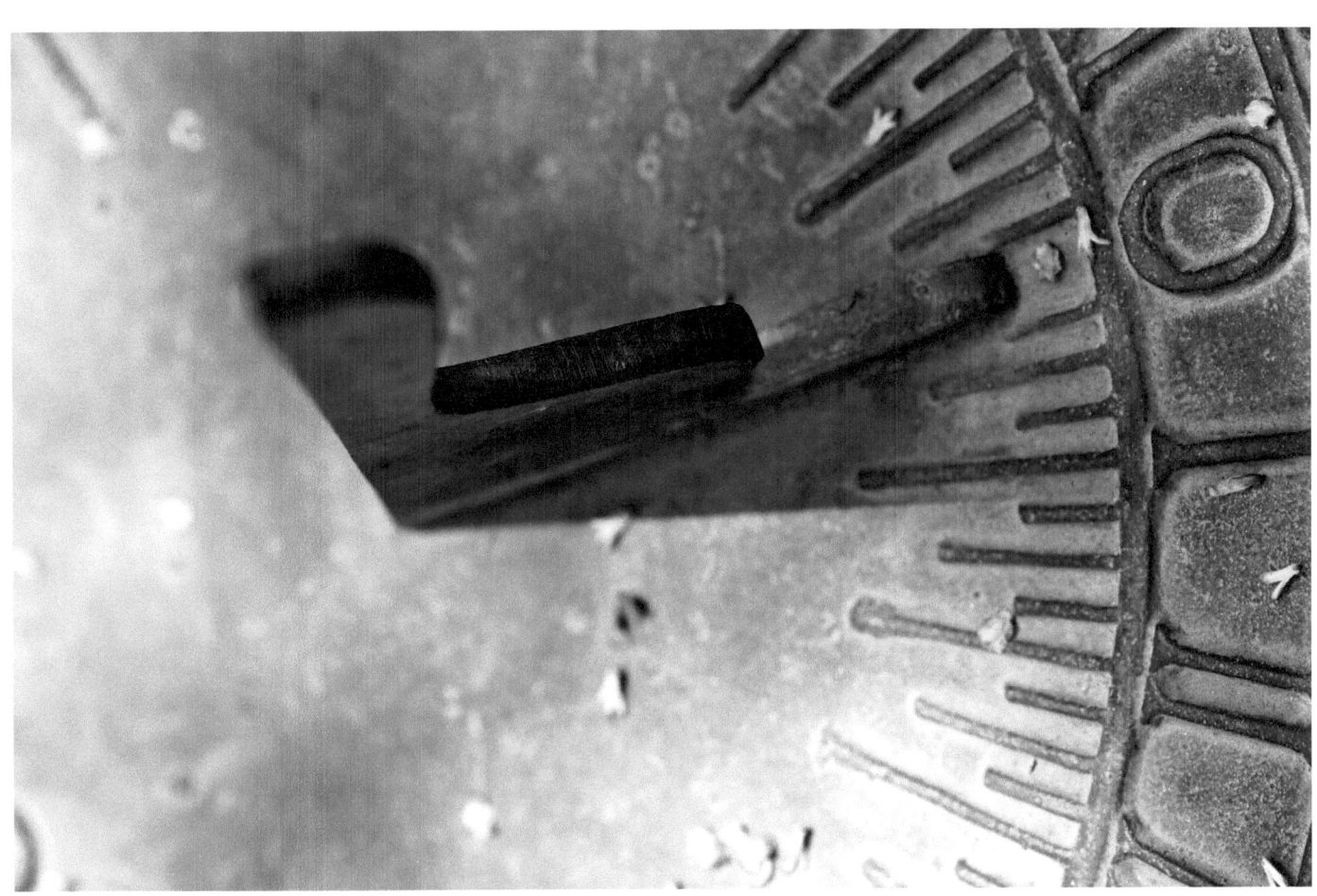

10002

www.ingramcontent.com/pod-product-compliance
Lightning Source LLC
Chambersburg PA
CBHW050736180526
45159CB00003B/1244